Advanc

Archi......g ...... r uture

"What's impressive is how Ravindar has not only articulated a case for 'Architecting your Future in the digital era' but also gives you the deep insights and examples to turn theory into practice. Best of all, he servers it up in an easy to understand, motivational and highly reliable manner."

—Sudesh Shah, VP,
Cloud and Strategy– SingTel, Singapore

"Awarded the Authority for Aspiring Entrepreneurs, and having been in the industry since before facebook, iPhone, Instagram, apps, or smart phones were even conceived, I see Ravindar's book as the next visionary jump in tech, It helps with implementation, learning, and a lot more. I have not worked with Ravindar, but I have seen him write this book, the precision he has used, the information which he has put together based on his experience, I would recommend any and every individual or company looking to further their overall bottom line and overall systems should connect with Ravindar."

—Naval Kumar, Entrepreneur,
Digital Marketing Expert, Author Ibiza, Spain

"It was pleasure reading the book (under publication)-'Architecting Your Future'. This is well written and logically compiled with practical examples. The book highlights the necessity and advantages of using technology to shape our future. This is one the Worth- Reading- Books for not only techies but other professional's comings from different fields and a common person, as well. I wish Mr. Ravinder Kumar, the author of the book, all the very best and GOOD LUCK."

—Dr. Sanjeev Kumar,
CEO & Managing Partner, Kumbra

"Thanks Ravi for sharing the copy of the book. I admire your work even though you have 24x7 job and you are frequent traveler. My comments about your work is: This book is based on proven and tested principles. I really like the pragmatic approach of clearly outlining step by step actions for the readers / Practitioner in pinning down their goals. In the current era of Digitalization and Digital enterprise, practitioner need to adopt quick changes not only in technology, business process adoption but also in organization (or individual) culture and mindset change, hence I highly recommend Architecting Your Future 'Why Technologists Triumph in a Generalist World.'"

—Sanjeev Agrawal, Advisor-Digital Transformation
Ex Director Service Management IBM India
and Ex CIO of IBM India &
mid-tier Insurance companies.

" 'Architecting Your Future' The brilliant though! A formidable piece of writing about real experience guaranteed to get you out of that rut and rethink your life's priorities in today's busy life. Full of action plans to stop procrastination and define purpose. Set you on the track to success and make you think how to build skills and talent stack to be success journey. Most recommended..."

—Navin Kumar Jaiswal,
HPE Chief Technologist,
Hybrid IT Practice AIPJ, Japan and Asia

"This book is amazing, and it is a privilege to write a testimonial for this. The author has demonstrated a coverage of all the topics, insights, questions and answers that anyone in their career would ask. I enjoyed the Life-Scale, Architecting, motivation and Energy chapters as it resonated to myself and immediately found as a source of new perspectives.

In summary a person can have at least 30 years working lifetime and this book is the source of 'accelerated learnings' of typical lifelong lessons for anyone to use as a tool to make their life and career a success."

—Tony Cadelina, Director,
SingTel, Asia Pacific

ARCHITECTING YOUR FUTURE

"Why Technologists Triumph in a Generalist World"

Discover Your 7 Tips, Technology and Strategies to Accelerate Your Success in Digital Era.

RAVINDAR KUMAR

Architecting Your Future

www.architectingyourfuture.com

Copyright © 2020 Ravindar Kumar

ISBN: 9798637413669

All rights reserved. No portion of this book may be reproduced mechanically, electronically, or by any other means, including photocopying, without permission of the publisher or author except in the case of brief quotations embodied in critical articles and reviews. It is illegal to copy this book, post it to a website, or distribute it by any other means without permission from the publisher or author.

Limits of Liability and Disclaimer of Warranty

The author and publisher shall not be liable for your misuse of the enclosed material. This book is strictly for informational and educational purposes only.

Warning – Disclaimer

The purpose of this book is to educate and entertain. The author and/or publisher do not guarantee that anyone following these techniques, suggestions, tips, ideas, or strategies will become successful. The author and/or publisher shall have neither liability nor responsibility to anyone with respect to any loss or damage caused, or alleged to be caused, directly or indirectly by the information contained in this book.

Medical Disclaimer

The medical or health information in this book is provided as an information resource only, and is not to be used or relied on for any diagnostic or treatment purposes. This information is not intended to be patient education, does not create any patient-physician relationship, and should not be used as a substitute for professional diagnosis and treatment.

Publisher
10-10-10 Publishing
Markham, ON
Canada

Printed in Canada and the United States of America

This powerful book will show you how to accelerate your success by focusing on small steps in your career— those little things that make the biggest difference.

This Book Is Perfect for You If:

You're serious about setting your career principles and having a system to achieve your goal. You have the dream, desire, and drive to create something bigger in your life, and to make an impact on your health, wealth, family, and your teams, making a greater world in the next digital machine age.

You are not only looking up to and following in the footsteps of high achievers, having a resilient career and **dual deep competency**, but you want to be one yourself, to define the growth mindset and build your future of success by knowing what would be your next *digital economy disrupters.*

You're constantly looking for new career-developing tools, frameworks, strategies, and techniques to help you increase your learning and productivity, gain clarity, become a better leader, and break through to new levels of success in all aspects of your life.

Whether you're a recent graduate, in mid-career, or are contemplating your performance in life or retirement—and whether it's time to make that big move, or you're just interested in making your current situation a little bit better—*Architecting Your Future* is your dynamic roadmap to building a joyful, fulfilling life that always holds the possibility of surprise, and a growth plan for your life.

This book is based on real experiences of industries, research, interviews, and best practices for the last 25 years. Success doesn't have an endpoint; it's experience and feeling. That's why you'll enjoy ongoing reading, training, and the application of goal setting strategies, building your inner circle, mentorship, and accountability, to empower you to quickly and consistently hit your goals and unlock success and growth.

Why: Architecting Your Future

Technology causes economic and personal transformation.

Discover Your Latest 7 Tips, Technology, and Strategies to Accelerate Your Success in the New Digital era

Key Take-Away:

What:

Tips-1: Talent Stack Platform (TSP): horizontal skills, vertical development – generalist to specialist to legend.

Tips-2: Goals: Prime motivation – Nothing happens without goals.

Tips-3: Energy Link with Performance: more energy, more money, more competency

Tips-4: Dual Deep Competency: technology with functional skills to grow and get success

Tips-5: Fast and Curious: Learn faster and be curious to get ahead.

Tips-6: Your Circle of Influencer and Your Associations

Tips-7: Digital Entrepreneur: Become a digital disrupter.

How:

Strategy-1: "CHFFRFAP" Career, Health, Fitness, Finance, Relationship, Family , Art and Play— DISCOVERY AND ASSESSMENT METHOD

Strategy-2: "4S-CDEF"—4 Self-Confidence, Discipline, Education and Reflection

Strategy-3: "UEDIC" MODEL (Understand, Explore, Develop, Implement, and Confirm)

7 Technology to Disrupt the world:

Technologies: IOT/IOE- Internet of Things / Internet of Everything, AI/MI-Artificial Intelligence and Machine Intelligence, 3D Printing, Block Chain, Virtual Reality/ Augmented Reality, Security and 5G.

MOVES FROM PROTECTOR TO DEFENDER TO HUNTER

Contents

Foreword... XV

Introduction.. 1

In recent years, you may have observed that computers are able to diagnose and predict diseases, drive cars, write your prescription, clean your floor, and even win Jeopardy in a new digital era.

1. Discover Your Life-Scale 23

When you have clarity of your quality of mind, and a bigger view, you will know how to understand, master, and regulate your emotional intelligence and intentions, and you will focus on your choice of career, health, finance, fitness, family, relationship, art and play.

2. Plotting 47

While trying to find your direction, you need to search for your purpose.

3. Constructing 61

The construction of your future means laying down your foundation for success, by developing and building skills, and practicing on a regular basis

4. Goals, Systems, and Focus 93

Your goals, system, and focus is like a three-dimensional viewpoint, and you need all three dimensions to be balanced to get real experience and optimum results. Strive to comprehend what will make you achieve goals by understanding driving forces which will convert your thoughts into behaviors and, ultimately, results.

4.1   Importance of Achieving Your Goal 110

4.2   Kinds of Goals 117

4.3   Career & Professional Goals 120

4.4   Health & Fitness Goals 133

4.5   Relationship Goals 147

4.6   Financial Goals 154

4.7   Family Goals 162

4.8   Art and Play Goals 168

**4.9   Goal Setting Do's & Don'ts:
         Awareness of Your Goals** 174

5. Architecting Lives 179

An architect always has a vision to see the complete picture, based on a goal. He applies architectural thinking to plan A and B, which includes a short-term goal to solve a problem, and a long-term strategy to achieve the desired outcome.

6. What Motivates You to Achieve Your Goals..........205

The key to successful goal setting is your ability to motivate yourself, keep the momentum, and stay motivated until you have achieved your goals.

**7. Energy Leads to Performance –
Time vs Energy vs Focus...211**

Time management is not a new subject. It is balance between time and energy, and focus in the best possible way in order to achieve our goals by producing results. This is called productivity.

**8. Energy, Physiology, Stress for
Goal Achievement...225**

The art of architecting your future is to have a talent stack platform of learning how to live, learn and love, to explore exponential growth in the digital era.

9. Your Inner Circle of Influence 233

Inner circle is not just about connecting with people but keeping the quality of your relationship with key team members, who will either influence you or be influenced and supported, reminding you from time to time how you are doing.

10. Get Digital, Get Hired..247

We are heading toward the most challenging territory of the future, called the digital era. Technology has decreased the demand for low-skilled workers, but at the same time it has increased it for highly skilled and knowledgeable workers globally.

11. Digitize Your Career.. **261**

Technology continues to disrupt industries and organizations, and provides an opportunity as well as forcing our careers to get disrupted. We have two choices: Either we wait and watch, or we become proactive to disrupt our future to be on the leading edge, and lead above average.

12. Seven Technology Disrupters for Future **271**

We continue living in an uncertain and complex world due to economical change with technological advancements

Conclusion **287**

Appendix - Activities and Diagrams........................... **297**

Glossary **303**

Acknowledgements **307**

References and Notes................................... **313**

About Ravindar... **319**

Foreword

Have you ever thought about your life purpose and architecting your future? Have you ever thought that it was time to transform your life, but didn't know how? There are probably lots of things you love doing, many things you want to experience, and goals you want to achieve. You may be dreaming of an extraordinary life, but your activities, obligations and commitments have nothing to do with your goals or dreams. You may be spending your life running faster and faster trying to keep up, and at the same time falling further and further away from living that extraordinary life about which you are dreaming.

To transform your life takes time, passion, goal, courage and a lot of self-awareness.

Ravindar Kumar is someone who has definitely overcome a life-changing event, and found a way into his own transformation. When he speaks you can sense that he has turned his life around; you know there is something different. Something resonates, and you know that what he is saying is true, even though you may not have heard it expressed in that way before. He wants you to live your life's purpose, architecting your future, being happy doing it, and feeling extraordinary every day.

In *Architecting Your Future*, you will find very simple ideas, guidelines and suggestions that you can follow to empower you to transform your life and start living the life you want to live. Start applying this now and move towards an extraordinary life.

Raymond Aaron
New York Times Bestselling Author

What you can expect from this book

❖ You have decided and are committed to do well and stand for excellence in your life of career, health, family, fitness, finance, relationship and art and play.

❖ Why technology is the single best innovation on the planet, to make your career successful. When you apply and adopt the technology you grow exponentially.

❖ How to use *Architecting Your Future* to set your goals, focus, and energy, to generate high performance and to be more productive.

❖ How to set your 7 dimensional goals to be successful and balanced your life.

❖ How to be more productive by managing your energy, to leverage time and emotion to lead your daily life.

❖ How dual deep competency, with technology, can instantly differentiate you from anyone who is struggling to sustain in their career.

❖ Why anyone can build skills in technology, and use them as a deep vertical development and competency tool to grow in next digital era.

❖ How to develop a fast and curious learning method, to learn less than 40 hours as a prototype, and then become an expert for living.

❖ What it takes to use a technology to brand yourself with massive credibility, in the next digital machine era, to become a legend and future leader

❖ The 3 steps to being successful in technology by becoming a *digipreneur.*

❖ 7 global key technologies of the future to make you a success and a disrupter the industries, to lead the future.

The target audience of this book INCLUDES:

❖ Students of Information, Science, communication and digital technology who want to be success in next digital era

❖ Students of specialized areas such as banking, manufacturing, healthcare, finance, telecommunication and enterprise, who want to build a dual deep competency strategy to be successful.

❖ Professionals working in private or global MNC of digital & communication who want to be high performers in their domain.

❖ Entrepreneurs who want to become digipreneurs in the digital era.

❖ Middle age professionals who get stuck in their career and don't know how to move on to the next level.

❖ Parents who want their kids to develop "TSP"-- talent stack platform the area of sports, professional, engineering, or education, and be prepared for the future.

❖ Academic and knowledge workers in colleges and universities, who want to be successful in next wave of the digital era with alignment with real industries experience.

❖ Technologists, IT specialists, architects, and engineers who want to become leaders in business.

Architecting Your Future Journey-Map

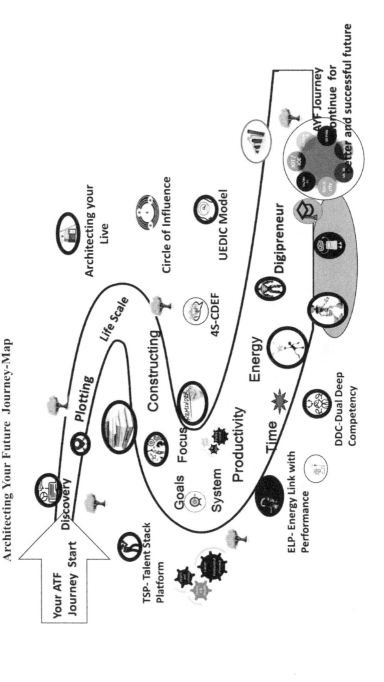

"EFFORTS and COURAGE are not enough without PURPOSE and DIRECTIONS for ARCHITECTING your FUTURE."

Introduction

F ive years from now, over one-third of skills (35%) that are considered important in today's workforce will have changed. The Fourth Industrial Revolution will have brought us advanced robotics and autonomous transport, artificial intelligence and machine learning, advanced materials, biotechnology, and genomics. These developments will transform the way we live, and the way we work. Some jobs will disappear, others will grow, and jobs that don't even exist today will become commonplace. What is certain is that the future workforce will need to align its skillset to keep pace in the next digital machine age.

Future of Jobs Report, World Economic Forum

DJ has been working in a global, multinational bank, for the last 13 years. Her experience is in consumer, retail, and corporate banking industries, having many industry certifications. She is doing extremely well in her career, and has been getting recognized for her quality of service in all the business units where she worked. She has given 100% of her time on jobs and work, moving from one business unit to another. But the main question arises: "Has she really grown in her career?" She is a scholarship holder and was very good in her academics. She also has a master's in information technology, as IT was booming, and everyone was recommending the IT sector more; hence, she decided to get a degree in IT. But she got her first break in the banking sector, which is one of the more prestigious and better careers for any woman to start with. She started liking her job, and she was growing and learning, with a lot of horizontal skills in her career; but she never thought that her vertical skill development growth was very constant. She worked hard for an organization and many business units, but she never worked hard for her personal growth. She was profoundly unhappy, as there was not much learning or long-term growth in her career after a certain period of time. She was only acquiring functional banking experience, and adding year after year of the same experience.

Limiting self-belief: My experiences and hard work will provide strong career growth (experience with expertise skills).

Reality: Having the work experience of doing the same job in an organization does not provide career growth. To grow in your career path, you need to acquire multiple skills, becoming more valuable for an organization, with a combination of adaptive education and experience.

John got his master's degree from one of the best universities in Australia. He worked with a global MNC for 20 years, in healthcare information technology and communication, in the area of operation and support. He has been working with a Fortune 100 company, in healthcare IT communication, and has always been proud, acquiring the best skills, knowledge, and experience in the world, but specializing in strategic operation management. He has grown very fast, from being an IT support engineer, to being the head of the operation business unit leaders. But due to globalization and resources alignment, his role has been made redundant and has shifted to the Philippines. He was suddenly asked one day to resign from the company or move to the Philippines, as his job had been consolidated and outsourced.

DJ and John are not the only one that are getting affected by globalization and technology innovation in digital disruption era. The researchers forecast that in the future, workforces in 2/3 of the world's population will be in the process of transitioning to a new techno-economy and digital machine era.

NEW DIGITAL MACHINE ERA

 Limiting self-belief: My specialized expertise will be relevant to industries, and will keep my job safe (Talent Stack Platform).

Reality: In today's digital economy, automation, robotics, and consolidation are the norm of job definitions. The Talent Stack Platform, with horizontal skills and vertical development, will be key to build talent; and it has to be relooked at, every 3 to 5-year life cycle. Today, all industries are getting disrupted; hence, everyone has to learn new skills in order to survive and grow.

I have always felt profoundly excited and fortunate to have had so much of my journey coincide with the growth of the information and digital technology in different industries of business. These remarkable information technology industries have provided me with all the challenges, learning opportunities, inspiration, and sense of purpose one could think of and ask for, as well as with friends and highly skilled colleagues across the globe. Yet the most interesting, challenging, and exciting times are clearly ahead of us.

The opportunities in the digital machine era—science, information, knowledge, technology, arts, sports, entertainments and business—are being created. They are being randomly and systematically brought to every human activity, creating entirely new living and career prospects that are destined to be architected by the next generation of technologies; and progressive collaboration with globally-minded individuals, from every part of the world is emerging. The self-initiatives of personalized education, research, exploring, and ability, to relearn, build, and scale, can make it possible for each of us to create the life we desire to pursue, and lead us toward the future and beyond.

 "Technology is a gift of god. After the gift of life, it is perhaps the greatest of god's gifts. It is the mother of civilizations, of arts and of sciences."

– Freeman Dyson

We know that there are challenges that come with today's digital and global business, hyper-converged information, and multi-cloud infrastructure, driverless cars, connectivity, and intense global competition. Our skills, knowledge, and life-long learning experiences need to better demonstrate how the digital entrepreneur (digipreneur) is addressing important industry and social concerns, such as enhancing the developing and emerging world, improving the environment, reducing inequality, modernizing the new digital world economy, building sustainable energy, and being innovative in finance, healthcare, education, transportation, personal security, and agriculture systems, for the next generation and the Digital and Machine era.

THINK LIKE AN ARCHITECT

Architecting your future, by applying an architectural thinking process, helps you start to envision, keeping the end goal in mind. The key is to start the process, and achieve your desired goal, step-by-step, in your life. Architects love the imagination, visualization, and setting up of a purposeful goal, and starting the process for planning and crafting, and reiterating the process, again and again, till they achieve the final goals. The question occurs: "What is the role of architects, and how can someone apply architectural thinking to the desired end goal—the design process of short-term achievement for human-centered problems—and apply the innovation technique to the "wicked problem" of designing your job, career, health, finance, and family, anticipating and imagining a better future for you and your family? By applying architectural thinking, we build what is required for the way we live, play, grow, and be successful in life.

The definition of an architect, from a building architect's point of view:

From Ayn Rand's book, *The Fountainhead:*

"He looked at the granite. To be cut, he thought, and made into walls. He looked at a tree. To be split and made into rafters. He looked at a streak of rust on the stone and thought of iron ore under the ground. To be melted and to emerge as girders against the sky.

These rocks, he thought, are waiting for me; waiting for the drill, the dynamite and my voice; waiting to be split, ripped, pounded, reborn; waiting for the shape my hands will give them."

Idea borrowed from "Becoming an Architect," by Lee W. Waldrep, Ph.D.

Word origin - 1550s, from Middle French *architect*, from Latin architects, from Greek *arkhitekton* **"master builder, director of works,"** from *arkhi-* "chief" (see archon) + *tekton* "builder, carpenter" (see texture). An Old English word for it was *heahcræftiga* **"high-crafter**."

There are a few things to be taken from that Rand quote. Note the repeated use of "**thought.**"
Was the character thinking about what the walls, rafters, girders, etc. would look like, and how they'd fit together, or was he thinking about how he would do the crafting and construction himself? Is he a "specialist" or an "architect?" What kind of thinking was he doing?
What does an architect do?
An architect doesn't just draw pictures and diagrams.

"In designing buildings, architects communicate with and assist those who have needs – clients, users and the public as a whole – and those who will make the spaces that satisfy those needs – builders and contractors, plumbers and painters, carpenters, and air conditioning mechanics." (Waldrep)

- **A large part of the role is about communication and fulfilling the purpose!**

- **Requirements gathering is huge – again, communication!**

"Architecture is the creation and communication of ideas. It is the creative and technical process for the design, management and construction of the built environment. It represents a collaboration and coordination with a broad range of experts to get a building built." – Robert D. Fox, AIA, IIDA, Principal, Fox Architects

So, what would happen if you put a carpenter, a plumber, an electrician, and an HVAC installer in a room and told them to build a house?

Architectural thinking is both a "top-down" and "bottom-up" approach to getting results, which matter to making your life meaningful.

A purpose orientation drives architectural thinking; systems, processes, and IT architecting is driven by requirements of purpose.

- Future architecting is driven by self-initiatives.

President Kennedy didn't say to build an Apollo 3-stage rocket and a Lunar Excursion Module.

- Useful purpose, affordable cost, acceptable period of time.

Useful purpose is predominant.

- The architect works with the client and the builder on problems and solutions. Part of architectural thinking comes from *insights and heuristics*.

- A chess master does not think many moves ahead; they see a pattern on the board, and they have the insight and experience to know the outcomes.

- Heuristics are codified, succinct expressions from lessons learned through your own observation or other's experience. Heuristics are a key tool of the systems architect.

  It's the same approach and framework required to architecting your future.

  ○ Success comes from wisdom.

  ○ Wisdom comes from experience.

  ○ Experience comes from mistakes.

- Good architects have deliberate practice, a lot of experience, and passion, and they have probably made a lot of mistakes and were willing to learn and re-learn with trend.

- As a result of the wisdom and mistakes, they have identified the patterns that work for the future. You need to anticipate your growth and vision. Now is the time to take vision to a massive action to drive a better future.

THINK LIKE A DESIGNER

The simple way to make *Architecting Your Future* become real is by executing like a designer. If you do things that are easier first, with a prototype, and follow step-by-step, keeping the bigger picture and goal in mind, then you can actually make a lot of progress in each step. You may find a strong purpose and enough reasons to design your future. The designer knows that the reason comes first, and that the results then follow. The reasons for doing well in your life—career, profession, family dream, or even social community—could be the motivation due to personal and societal reasons. People want to do well because they want to make their personal, professional, and social life more meaningful and successful. There could be family reasons; people want to do better things for other people, to achieve in their career, and support and make the future better and sustainable for others.

Every person in the world devotes countless hours to thinking about their future, and trying to solve their problems and their present situation in life. Almost everyone wishes that they could change something in their life. Whether it's family life, friendships, other relationships, or finances, everyone wants to change something, and this is a strong reason people have for designing the future. The way to do that is to seek clarity and purpose in life—to know why designing your future is important—and then set your goal.

The goal will help you to overcome all kinds of challenges that you face daily in your personal and professional life. However, many of us are great at trying to set goals, but most of us are practically incapable of following through with them. Think about it. How many times have you decided on a course of action, and simply didn't follow through with it? That is pretty much the norm for most people. Sometimes even setting goals at all is harder than accomplishing any. The easiest way of looking at this is to think of each and every New Year's Eve. The largest part of New Year's celebrations are not the parties and the get-togethers; it is actually in the resolutions.

As much as we all like to attend and talk about New Year's Eve parties, the most common source of conversation is the resolutions for a new year.

It is really just code talk for new goals that need to be set. The only problem is that most of us set the same resolutions every year, and year-on-year, we are unsuccessful. After all, if we were successful, why would we need to keep making the same resolutions year after year?

Designing your future will give you a sense of direction, and direction will help you reach your destination. Without direction, in a year, or in 5 years or 10 years, I am sure you will reach somewhere, but I'm not sure where. So, designing your future, and applying architectural thinking, will help you to build a purposeful and meaningful life.

This book will help you to assess, discover, and design your future, and will provide direction. It will teach you how to end the constant need to re-set the same resolutions every year. Basically, this book will be your comprehensive design guide to setting and fulfilling goals in every aspect of your life, and tracking and accomplishing them by applying architectural thinking as long-term objectives, and a design thinking process as short-term objectives.

When I say every aspect of your life, I mean *every* aspect of your life. Aren't you getting tired of trying to set goals for yourself, and always finding that you have to do it again almost every other month? With this, you will develop and learn major dimensions of life, and each dimension requires agile thinking and an iterative process. Agility can help you apply and observe directly, which will give you significant results. The iterative process can be applied indirectly in case you think your goal is not working, as per your initial plan, and not getting enough results. This can also apply if you think it isn't giving you meaningful results as per your expectations; you can go back and re-position as per your plan, and you can change it without affecting others in the process. There are two types of goals and processes required to design your future. One is long-range goals, which are your future and dream goals; the other is short-range goals, which are for today, tomorrow, next week, next month, or next year. Our goals should be a list of personal development, as well as economic, finance, personal, health, wealth, career, professional success, and social development. These can come with the pain of losing, or the joy of winning. Losing is painful— but if you achieve it, then you can congratulate yourself and celebrate with your family and friends.

Many people work hard on their jobs but don't work enough on themselves and on their futures, and what they desire to become. If you are working hard on your job, you make your living; but if you are working harder on yourself and your future, then you make your fortune. So working harder is involved in making your plan and aligning your plan with purpose. You can observe yourself moving forward and growing, by:

Step 1: Discovering your life scale.

Step 2: Finding the priorities of the purpose and meaning of your life.

Step 3: Assessing your speedometer of life, and analyzing.

Step 4: Discovering, setting up, identifying, and writing down your key goals and game plan. (Writing a goal shows that you are serious. Everybody thinks that things will get better, but it will only happen if you prepare and plan, take a risk and an action, and move forward.)

Step 5: Checking the size of your goal and the kind of goal, which affects your future. (You are affected by your goals every day. Sometimes making dual goals with dual competency makes sense; in case your first choice doesn't work out, you have an alternative.)

Step 6: Setting up energy, attention, and focus on a system, as you know that energy links with performance.

Step 7: Choosing a platform to build your strong foundation through a **Talent Stack Platform (TSP)**. TSP does not provide immediate results but a foundation and alignment of your long-term goals, to make change appropriate and meaningful. You are always motivated to do more with TSP.

Step 8: Choosing to become a *digipreneur* in the new digital machine era, so that you can accelerate your career even in tough and uncertain times.

"Choose a job you love, and you will never have to work a day in your life."

— **Confucius**

COMBINING ARCHITECTURAL THINKING WITH A DESIGN MINDSET

Combining architectural thinking with a design mindset is a method of thinking big. It is keeping the end goal in mind and applying a design principle to consider the outcomes as a result, and refining with deliberate practice, and fine-tuning as you feel appropriate. Architectural thinking is used most of the time when you want to build the solution to any problem in industries. This has been adopted for many years, and it is very well aligned with a design mindset to get best results.

By combining, you get the following outcomes:

People Who Use Architecting For Their Future, Effectivly Set A System With Goals.

To keep an architecture-thinking mindset, following a design process and achieving the goal is the way to keep progressing forward, and to:

- Know where you are heading in your life.

- Have a purpose in life and focus better on one or two key goals, to drive with objective and results.

- Show more self-confidence as you see promise in your future, and you believe in it.

- Perform better in all areas of life on the life scale (CHFFRFAP Model) to start with.

- Suffer less from stress, anxiety, and distractions, and concentrate your energy to make daily life worth living.

- Align horizontal skills and vertical development to be better equipped to challenge complexity, automation, volatility, and uncertainty in the world. (Future skills require strong TSP.)

- Become what you like, and be more successful in life by building your circle of influencers.

- Align and personalize your digital disruptive skills to become a *digipreneur* for the new digital machine era and global economy, to be ahead with others.

- Be happier and more satisfied with life and family, and give back more to society.

 "If you do not step forward in your life, you will always be in the same place."

FUTURE WORKFORCE

In recent years, you have observed that computers have learned to diagnose and predict diseases, drive cars, write your prescription, clean your floor, and even win jeopardy. They can write a book for you, cook your food, and dispense and deliver at your door step. They can follow your instructions, and instruct you back with correction steps in case if you do the wrong thing. It means that the machine has started learning from you and is challenging you back. In an advancement like this, it creates unprecedented economic bounty, creating new jobs in the market, but at the same time, it is a threat to human economy, and forces you to reinvent and rethink. Despite huge technological changes in economy, globalization, and advancement, middle class income has stagnated and is still going in downwards trends across developed and developing nations, and a share of the population's jobs has fallen, and continues to fall. MIT Professors, Andrew McAfee and Eric Brynjolfsson, reveal the technological force driving this reinvention of our economy. In recent times, technology has been creating a path toward future prosperity of art and science together, and has required us to be technology empowered and socially enabled for a future-ready task force of 2 billion, under the age of 20. In every industry, whether it is manufacturing, agriculture, or high tech, there is a call of action to all workforces to become digital entrepreneurs, to survive and be successful in the next digital machine era.

In the digital era, research tells us two important things to watch for in the future:

a. Technology professionals value innovation projects and learning new skills above everything else (including wages and job security).

b. There is little progress in the participation of women in technology globally.

A WELL-ARCHITECTURED LIFE

A well architectured future makes sense in life. It's a life where you know who you are, what your purpose is, your life objective, what you believe, and what you dream of for your future. When you have well-architectured your future, and you look back at yourself, you will have satisfaction. If someone asks you what is happening in your life, you will have the answer, and you will know where you are heading in life. You can respond to people that your life is going well, and tell them how and why.

A well-architectured future is your personal portfolio of experience, adventure, and learning, as well as of failures that taught you the importance of designing and planning lessons, setting up objectives and goals, and being hardworking, which made you stronger and helped your future be better and more progressive. It's worth analyzing and emphasizing that failure, and knowing your strengths and weaknesses in your life, to have a well-architectured future.

By having a well-architectured future, and setting goals and measuring your achievements, you are able to see what you have done and what you are capable of. The process of achieving goals, and seeing their achievement, gives you the confidence and the belief in yourself that you need, to be able to achieve higher and more difficult goals. Providing that you have the self-discipline to carry it through, goal setting is also relatively easy.

We are going to help you figure out what the well-architectured future of your life looks like for you in the next digital era, and in the global knowledge economy. My colleagues, peers, students, and clients tell us that it's fun to anticipate the future and be ready. They also tell us that it's full of new surprises, awareness, and images while setting up systems and goals. Achieving them step-by-step, and creating meaningful dream careers, looks and feels like you are living in a science fiction life, which you never imagined could be possible so soon. We can assure you that at times, in the future, you will be out of your comfort zone. We are going to ask you to do things that you may not have thought to do in your past, and to have confidence in the future, or at the very least to see the difference from what you have been taught in the past.

Living your dream life is becoming a reality.

Self-assess where you are now, and where you will be in the next 1, 3, or even 5 years, and which direction to choose in regard to your priority and purpose, for a better future.

- How can Talent Stack Platform help you to keep experience, education, and exposure future-ready?

- Which kind of system do you need to build to achieve your goals and align with your inner circle?

- Have self-awareness of your personal development by building your fast and curious learning, to keep up with the technology pace.

- How can you collaborate with your inner circle association for success?

- How do you link your energy with performance? How do you manage your positive energy, emotions, and your feelings, to keep time, attention and focus?

Choose disrupter technology to look forward to your digital machine era.

These are the systems, processes, and mindsets. What happens when you do these things? What happens when you engage in *architecting your future?* Actually, you start feeling that you are aware of the future, and it's quite an extraordinary feeling, which changes your behavior, habits, and association. Things you are thinking about will start to show up and pull you toward your purpose, of your job, career, dreams, and goals in your life. You will start hearing about opportunities, friends who want to work with you, job openings that you are looking for, and you will get associated with people with the same dreams and desires as yours.

You will start exploring, reading, learning, researching, and developing your personal philosophy and goals, and meeting with the people who are willing to work with you in your architecting, to design your future journey. You start feeling energized and "lucky" because of moving from a fixed mindset to a flexible and growth mindset. Your purpose is your well designed future, goals, awareness, performance, results, energy, attention, and time management.

In addition, there is the process of assessment, to find out who you are and how you want to make your life meaningful. What you want has an impactful effect on your future. There will be significant efforts and massive actions required, but rather surprisingly, everyone will help you. And by being aware of the process, you will have fun and will have great achievement of self-satisfaction and self-confidence.

The process of architecting your future will be a self-guide to support you and challenge you. You are going to have ideas, fun tools, methods, and processes for your architecting, to design your future by setting up your system and goals, to find new job skills and a new career, and to help with health, finance, personal economy, relationships and growing skills, for the next big things in your life, which you will love as you enjoy your success.

 "The greatest discovery is that a human being can alter his life by altering his attitude of his mind."

– **William James**

DISCOVER
"KNOWING YOURSELF IS THE
BEGINNING OF WISDOM."
– ARISTOTLE

Discover
Your Life-Scale

CHAPTER 1

START WITH PRIORITY ON PURPOSE

Nobody teaches you how to discover your true self, because there is no character development theory available, except behavior science profiling methodology. When you have clarity of your quality of mind, and a bigger view, you will know how to understand, master, and regulate your emotional intelligence and intents, and you will focus your choice, which drives you to your best destination in life. Clarity of mind and a bigger view empowers you to overcome the frustration and challenges caused by putting time and effort into the wrong things. It also enables you to be the best in your career growth, and to be a compatible partner and friend in your business, and with your parents, children, and friends, and the people around you.

Architecting your future requires you to have a 60ft view from above, and an understanding of where you are. This will help you to understand your present state, as well as how to kick-start to start building to your future state—where are you? How far can you reach? What obstacles do you need to face? How well are you prepared? How will you track your progress and measure it to be successful and joyful?

"You can't stay in your corner of the forest, waiting for others to come to you. You have to get to them sometime."

—Pooh, A. A. Milne.

The importance of architecting your future requires you to understand where you are. You need to understand and break down your life structure into some discrete areas: professional career and job, health and fitness, relationships, family, spiritual, social, and cultural. These are all integral parts of your life, and all these are linked to each other to achieve your goals and be successful. As we have said, we will only focus on personal and professional career development, but you won't be able to understand how to architect your future until you understand how it fits in with the rest of your life, and how you can connect the dots together to enrich your life experience. So, in order to start where you are now, with what you are and what you have achieved so far, you must do a self-assessment of your current situation, and be able to articulate your future goals. If someone asks how your life is going, you should be in the position to respond optimistically, and to say that it is going fantastic. Research demonstrates that optimistic people are more successful, healthier, and live longer. Let's examine each of the 5 dimensions briefly.

5D Assess Architecting Your Future

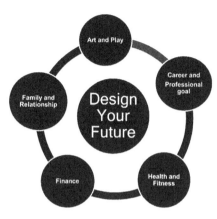

By Architecting your future with setting your goals you can:
- Achieve more in your lifetime
- Improve your overall performances in life
- Increase your motivation to achieve the most out of your life
- Increase your pride and satisfaction in your achievements
- Improve your self-confidence
- Plan to eliminate attitudes that hold you back and cause unhappiness

Job, Career, and Profession: Everyone is wondering how they can hope to survive in today's harshly competitive, technology-centered, globalization market. A lot of time is spent thinking about careers, and the preparation and participation in the great, on-going and exciting adventures in our lives. It does not matter which stage of life you are in, whether you are studying, preparing for college, or looking for a job, or whether you are an experienced professional or are retired. Most people have more than one form of career objective or plan at one time, and continue building processes to be better and better every day. We always want to be our best, and assessing our current state is important in order to know how we are doing, as well as acknowledging our accomplishments. Companies are outsourcing work to people thousands of miles away, who produce high quality work for a fraction of the cost. Soon, artificial intelligence and digital machines will be powerful enough to replace truck drivers, bank tellers and agents, technical support, language translators, accountants, tax consultants, and all jobs that don't require creativity. To become irreplaceable in today's job, career, and professional marketplace, we need to attend and become a master. If you become a master, you will unlock higher intelligence, rare skills, and creative ability that will be hard to outsource, and difficult to automate in the digital era.

Health and Fitness: People recognize that health and fitness is the most important aspect of their lives, and consider it as a platform or foundation for all their success. By *health and fitness*, I don't mean your annual health checkup; it's about how strong you're physical, mental, emotional, and spiritual health is, and how you are now ready and willing to apply tactics to take challenges in your life. How do you see the importance of your health and fitness in regard to architecting your future?

Finance: Finance and personal economy play a key role in everyone's lives. Becoming financially independent is everyone's goal in life. Who doesn't want financial independence so that they can live their life better? Money is not only a key motivational factor to architecting your future, but it gives you choice and freedom in what you do in your life.

Family: Family is all about happiness and support. Family is a powerful reason for many of us to do well in our lives, and it makes life meaningful. Jim Rohn said, *"Your family and your love must be cultivated like a garden. Time, effort, and imagination must be summoned constantly to keep any relationship flourishing and growing."* Assessing your current state is important so that you can be balanced while architecting your future for success.

Relationship: Relationships play a critical role in life, and there are two parts: Inwardly, it is the relationship with yourself, and the relationship with your family, friends, and community. Outwardly, it is the relationship with your external world, such as your colleagues, in professional and social circles. We have to balance these relationships in order to sustain, survive, enjoy, grow, and have fun. There are two sides of the coin: One is your inner-circle, and the other is your outer circle—when you combine them together, it becomes more valuable to your life.

Art & Play: We all know that art, sports, and playing makes our lives joyful, colorful, and playful. We all love it. Art is often understood in terms of play, fun, and nature. Playing is a behavior that is performed in order to enjoy our capacity of being able to perform and be better for ourselves. The more difficult the task, the greater the pleasure and fun. That is why playing is comparative in essence in every game. The player can compare his performance with that of himself or of others. Play is then unfolding into a contest. The introduction of other players allows the degree of difficulty to be raised: The players can hinder each other in reaching their goals, exemplary in football or chess, and that makes our lives more enjoyable, giving us a sense of achievement. This isn't a tangible way to measure, and is relatively subjective, but it gives us self-fulfillment and can be measured by satisfaction, enjoyment, life-span and an association with wellbeing.

What if some of your friends ask you how your life is going?

I remember, since my childhood till now, a most interesting question that was asked very frequently by my friends and family: "How is your life going?" And your answer comes promptly from your conscious mind. Let's do an assessment to help you answer this promptly, and to discover yourself. You know where you are heading in designing your future roadmaps, but before that, you need to appreciate and acknowledge your achievements so far, whatever that may be, in regard to your job, career, health and fitness, relationships, spirituality, art, and play. Please highlight, note, and recognize your achievements from your past. Now you are required to look forward, which is the key to architecting your future, and you can apply a pragmatic approach method toward goals.

The activity below is going to help you to know where you are, how to architect your future, and what you need to prepare, plan, and process in order to build a successful journey. You need to recognize what you have accomplished. You will not know where you are going until you know where you are at in your present position or situation— I call this self-gratitude.

SELF-GRATITUDE

Self-gratitude is about being grateful for yourself, what you have, and the life around you.

Note: Please highlight all the major accomplishments related to your education ranking, career, health, wealth, house, kids, education, relationships, achievements (medals, scholarships, sports, or social achievements), social services, support of NGO works, etc.

Note: Do this exercise to recognize being self-effacing, and acknowledge your accomplishments to have self-respect and gratitude.

Name five things that you have accomplished that you are proud of so far.

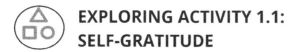 **EXPLORING ACTIVITY 1.1: SELF-GRATITUDE**

Accomplishment(1)

Accomplishment(2)

Accomplishment(3)

Accomplishment(4)

Accomplishment(5)

As you have written with your gratitude, you can feel relaxed and be thankful to yourself.

Recent research shows that you need 7 ingredients, or 7 pillars that stand for success in life, and are required for a balanced approach to being happy and joyful.

Let's try to understand what those 7 ingredients in

life are. This is what I call the CHFFRFAP Model in this book, which is to observe, analyze, and improve on your current situation, and to see how many points you score while getting to your current state and future scale of your meaningful journey. I would like to share the best quote I have ever read and said in TED by Andrew Mcafee, Professor and Researcher from MIT which I have applied in my life:

 "The world is intresting place, and my job is to go explore it."

Once you find an interest in yourself and others, you are going to be unstoppable, and that is the reason I have created the Speedo Meter Method of Success, which is an assessment of your career, health, finances, fitness, relationships, and art and play. You can decide at what speed and what pace, and how far you want to travel in your life scale. This tool is for you to plan your future and to set your coverage of your life scale, and you can revisit it when you feel you have achieved it.

THE LIFE SCALE SPEEDO METER

(For career, health, fitness, finance, relationships, family, art and play)

The speedo meter will gage your current situation and status so that you can be aware and know how to build and plan to architect your future. To take an assessment of your current situation, at your chosen speed and intensity, use the Life Scale Speedo Meter (CHFFRFAP Method).

C = Career
H = Health
F = Fitness
F = Finance
R = Relationship
F = Family
A =Art
P = Play

This is like the architecture of your *life's wheels*— the wheels driven by the speedo meter as a method of measurement.

As you know, to drive a car smoothly, and to achieve optimum speed and comfort, you need to align and balance your wheels on a regular basis.

You know where you are, at what speed you can accelerate, how you can maintain your maximum speed, and how far you can go with mileage. If you want your life to go smoothly, then you need to choose and balance your life wheel, to be of equal number and size of each and every aspect of your life.

The rule is that if you want to go at a higher speed in life, then you need a bigger wheel size to achieve a higher number in the LIFE SCALE SPEEDO METER (CHFFRFAP).

This is your basic foundation and rule to understand yourself better:

The wheels consist of 5 main areas of your life's importance, and you should consistently score at least a 2 or

3 in these areas. Eventually, your goals should be a higher number in each of your personal growth areas.

You can score from 1 to 5, 1 being the minimum score, and 5 being the desired score.

My recommendation is that "the higher the number, and the bigger the wheel, the better your life performance will look."

1.1 SPEEDO-SUCCESS METER

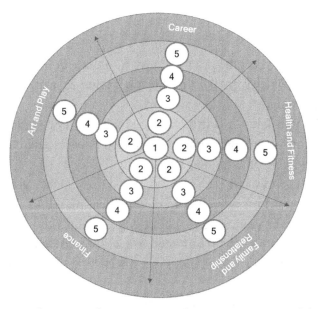

This speedo-Meter will give your gage of your current status and then you know how your build and plan your Architecting your future

Limiting self-belief: I am doing very well in my life and may not need to work hard.

Reality: You cannot do well in your life if you don't have a DREAM, DESIRE, PASSION, and VISION for your life, or if you are not able to start early and manage every aspect of your life.

The long-term success that you need to attend depends on the roundness of important traits of the CHFFRFAP Scale Speedo Meter, which focuses on each aspect of life as a pragmatic approach. The higher the number in each area, the better and easy the journey to achieve your goal successfully. The larger the wheel size, the faster you can accomplish your goals.

I am going to recommend that you assess your career, health, fitness, family, relationships, finances, and art and play. Health and fitness is the foundation and base of your life architecture because, as you know, if your health is not in your control, your life will go out of control; so giving attention to your health will be key to achieving your goals and running your life smoothly. Your career, family, relationships, finances, and art and play will all depend on your good health and fitness.

I want to highlight that there is no perfect balance of each area, and that it is based on your age, time, priority, and lifestyle. In our lives, at different times and stages, all have different requirements and goals. We have different levels of health, and different careers and interests.

Kok Leong is a young, single person, fresh out of college and having an abundance of physical health. She has a lot of art and play, as well as her career to focus on, but no meaningful relationship yet, and no financial freedom. A married couple with 2 children have lots of art and play compared to a single person. In comparison, Kok Leong's CHFFRFAP wheels would look different from this couple's. As we grow, our personal and social responsibilities change, and our priorities change, and we are more concerned with health, fitness, and finances. Take the example of Kok Leong's CHFFRFAP success wheel, and observe what it looks like.

Kok Leong's current assessment shows that she has good health and fitness, but she also needs to balance her career and finances, with a development plan to balance her routine. In regard to her relationships, they will improve as she progresses in her life.

1.2 KOK–LEONG ACCESS CURRENT LIFE SUCCESS WHEEL

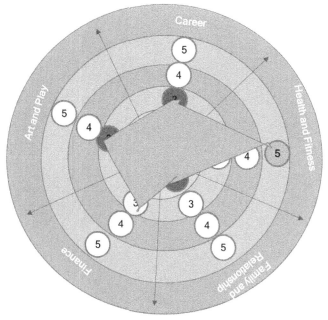

This speedo-Meter will give your gage of your current status and then you know how your build and plan your Architecting your future

Dr. Raj is another example. Dr. Raj is a medical doctor with an MBA. He is well educated in medicine and business, and lives with his wife and two kids in the United States. He has had the secure position of being a practicing healthcare partner for 10 years, in California, USA. He works for a Fortune 100 ICT company, with worldwide experience to manage healthcare clients. He is well balanced with career growth, health and fitness, family, relationships, and art and play, each having the highest score of 5. This indicates that he has a well-balanced and coherent life style.

1.3 DR-RAJ ACCESS CURRENT LIFE SUCCESS WHEEL

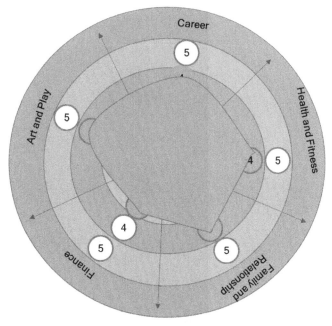

This speedo-Meter will give your gage of your current status and then you know how your build and plan your Architecting your future

Your Career Speedo Meter

In your career is where you spend most of your time thinking, planning, and reiterating, again and again. As you progress, your career goals and desires change. This diagram is intended to make you realize that no matter what stage you are at in your career, you need to analyze, plan, and decide to move forward.

1.4 CAREER SPEEDO METER

This speedo-Meter will give your gage of your current status and then
you know how your build and plan your Architecting your future

Your Health and Fitness Speedo Meter

As you know, health is the foundation to all success.
Health means not only physical health; it's also about your
mental health, your inner health, and how you feel about
your past and your future. It's about how much faith and
belief you have in your current and future health plan. If
you can see promise in your future, you will be able to do
anything to architect your future, in order to support, build,
and achieve your health goals.

1.5 HEALTH AND FITNESS SPEEDO METER

This speedo-Meter will give your gage of your current status and then you know how your build and plan your Architecting your future

Your Family and Relationship

As you know, family support, and our relationship with family and the outside world, is the key to making our life successful long term—and the bigger benefit and impact is good health. Researchers have studied health trajectories, including triumphs and failures in regard to career and marriage, and the findings produced startling results.

1.6 FAMILY AND RELATIONSHIP SPEEDO METER

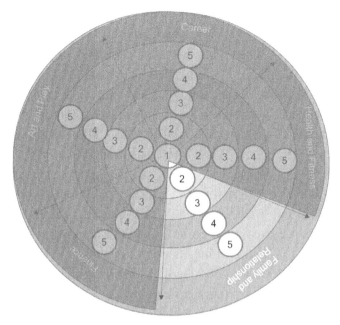

This speedo-Meter will give your gage of your current status and then you know how your build and plan your Architecting your future

"The real surprising finding is that our relationships and how happy we are in our relationships has a powerful influence on our health," said Dr. Robert Waldinger, a psychiatrist at Massachusetts General Hospital, and Professor of Psychiatry at Harvard Medical School, and director of the study.

Your Finances

Finances and personal economy play a key role in everyone's lives, especially when having to deal with money responsibly when focusing on your career and growth—and when you don't have deep pockets, which requires planning, restraint, and patience. It also takes a certain amount of self-knowledge, discipline, and desire to succeed. One of the basic questions to acknowledge is whether you have financial dreams, financial goals, or financial freedom. While this may sound like the same repetitive question, it's not the same. Financial dream is something you hope for; a financial goal is something you plan for; and financial freedom is something you fight for. And it's the execution, committing, and planning—not the hoping—that makes things happen for you.

I have described in detail, in later chapters, what a financial goal looks like, and how you achieve it.

The financial success wheel, below, is an assessment tool to help you understand your current financial status, and to define your goal so that you can plan, execute, and achieve your financial freedom.

1.7 FINANCE SPEEDO METER

This speedo-Meter will give your gage of your current status and then
you know how your build and plan your Architecting your future

This is a self-assessment based on the speedo meter. This
is not to showcase or to share with anyone; it's your own,
and you need to be honest with yourself to achieve the best
results for you.

Your Art and Play

Art and play is the key to having more fun, enjoyment,
and satisfaction in your life daily. Without art and play,
your life becomes purposeless. Art and play can be used
as a means of fun, entertainment, learning, dedication,
advertising, and showing one's personality and talent.

Without art, our world would be very dull, boring, and uninteresting, if you think about it. It plays a significant role in our lives. Art and play has a very important role in the digital machine era and modern society.

1.8 ART AND PLAY SPEEDO METER

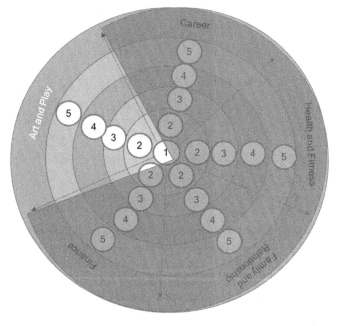

This speedo-Meter will give your gage of your current status and then you know how your build and plan your Architecting your future

Once you have identified each area of improvement, and your current situation in each area, then we can move to the next level to understand your life scale, career, and work and dream view, and how it works together as an integrated approach. And a most interesting question to ask yourself is: Does it complement or clash with the purpose of your life and future?

Quick Summary

In discovering your life, we have gone through the importance of gratitude and your past achievements to acknowledge your past and look in to the future. Self-gratitude is about being grateful for yourself, what you have, and the life around you. We have identified the tool called the Speedo Meter Success Wheel, to align your path from your current situation to your future state, giving importance to each aspect of your life—career, health, fitness, family, relationship, finance, art, and play (CHFFRFAP). You can analyze your current state and set your goals to your future state, based on your priorities and purpose, which can be from as short as 3 months, to as long as 1, 3, or 5 years, to enjoy your journey of *architecting your future.*

EXPLORING ACTIVITY 1.2: CAREER/HEALTH/FITNESS/FAMILY/ RELATIONSHIP/FINANCE/ART/ PLAY (CHFFRFAP-SPEEDO METER)

1. Write down your accomplishments so far in the areas of career, health, fitness, relationship, finance, and art and play.
2. Write down your understanding about career, health, fitness, relationship, finance, and personal economy and associations, and how you feel about art and play.
3. Write down your architecture view of your life, and whether you would like to work on any area that would help you to achieve your career and professional developments goal.
4. Try your assessment on the CHFFRFAP Model, and see which kind of map you generate. Have fun and reflect on yourself, and recognize and apply gratitude and self-empathy.

   Note: Self-recognition is a sense of maturity, and self-empathy is motivation.

Note your current status, and challenge yourself to improve in all aspects of your life. Self-analyze after 1 to 3 years, and see what kind of shape you are able to make it.

"A mind troubled by doubt cannot focus on the course to victory."

—**Arthur Golden**

Plotting

P lotting your future means finding a direction to reach your target destination. While trying to find the direction, you need to search for your purpose. There has been significant research done in the past about purpose and its powerful tools. Your purpose is your goal and objective that matters most to you. Your purpose drives you to become purposeful. Being purposeful is applying your best self to achieve the most that matters to you. For example, what do you look like when you are at your best? What are the two or three words that best describe you? Or how do you look when you're at your very best at work and at home, and what do you like the most? When you apply yourself to be your best, whether you're at work or at home, or at a sports or social event, then you become purposeful. Purposeful people always have greater wellbeing, and they achieve more in their lives. Take the example of being purposeful and plotting. The plotting system is mostly used in maritime navigation or aviation communication, and is used to find the visibility based on your desired destination, and you can communicate throughout your journey. It is the process of directing watercraft to a destination, in a safe and expeditious manner, from a known present position. A course is determined, which avoids the dangers; and on this course, estimates are made on time schedules. The task is to periodically make route checks and required adjustments as you progress toward your destination. The method used depends on the type of ship (vessel), its role, and its mission.

Architecting your future also requires some level of mechanism to plot and go through the communication process to arrive at your destination. Plotting your life through a radar and communication system will have a few questions regarding your identification, who you are, what your position is, and what your vision and mission is, so that you can navigate and control your route, and you do not clash with other ships on your success path.

Who are you? Knowing yourself and identifying your purpose is the key to being on the path of success.

What do you believe? What are the key values to you and your family?

To what degree do you tune into your life for success? What you tune into will lead you in the direction you want.

Which direction have you set for your life (e.g. joy, fun, spiritual, social, etc.)?

What are you doing to achieve your life-scale, work-scale, and dream-scale? And how are these dots connecting in the future? Are they linked together to share a better Speedo Meter of success?

Limiting self-belief: I am doing very well in my life and may need to work hard or build alternative skills.

Reality: The speed of change is faster than it ever has been in history. You cannot do well in your career, and still maintain a proper pace, if you are no longer able to manage every aspect of your life.

Plotting your future to find direction and meaning means identifying each dimension, and defining and personalizing each area to set your directions. As you know, you need identification and purpose for your life. What you want to become in your life is more important than what you will achieve in your life-view, work-view, and dream-view of your journey.

So let's discuss and understand more about some of the harder points of your life, and to what degree you should tune into these, and in which direction you should set your life. It is not hard to assess, prepare, and plan if you have the proper tools, process, and method to kick-start your journey and carefully navigate rather than thinking, worrying, and not taking any actions to improve and achieve. I have created experience, and hundreds of pages of research work done on how you take your life-scale, career-scale, and dream-scale challenges, to motivate your thinking and how you feel, and to improve your performance, as seen in the diagram below.

2.1 ARCHITECTURAL THINKING SCALE
(Dream, Career, And Life-Scale)

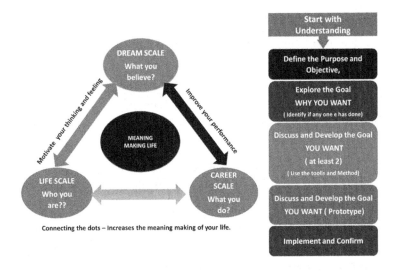

Connecting the dots – Increases the meaning making of your life.

You need three things to plot your Speedo Meter Success Wheel: life-scale, work-scale, and dream-scale.

The best way to achieve your goal, and connect these dots together, is by understanding, plotting, reading, reviewing, measuring, progressing, playing, enjoying, and living a meaningful life.

Life-Scale:

Your life-scale is your long-term objectives, correspond-ing to work with your dream-scale and how you see yourself as a success. You may not have a clear understanding and be able to articulate yourself, as not everyone has clarity of their life-scale point, but as you progress, you will have clarity. A life-scale is about your thoughts, your feelings, and how you see the world and your scale. The clearer your life-scale, the more valuable you become. Your life-scale is like two sides of one coin—it has an inward and an outward scale. *Inward* is related to your inner circle: yourself, your family, your community, and your friends; whereas *outward* means how the world sees you. What does money, fame, and professional and personal accomplishment have to do with the successful exploring and experiences of life? It will help to find out, and once you have written down your life-scale, then you need to plot and plan for your work-scale point, and how you connect to your dream-scale.

Our life-scale can be simple, thoughtful, selfless, and respectful to ourselves and to society.

Your life-scale point reflection is your thinking and your desired outcomes that matter most to you and your family.

The following questions will help you to self-analyze and find the meaning for your life and your life-scale, and it doesn't mean that you need to do research.

As Rachel Reman said,

"Often, finding meaning is not about doing things differently; it is about seeing familiar things in new ways."

So:

What is the meaning and purpose of life?

What is the relationship between the individual, family, friends, and works?

What is a good life-scale definition for you and your family?

What is your spritual scale, and how does it affect your career?

How does it affect your art and play in your life?

It's interesting to know how Bill and Belinda Gates impacted the whole world and spread the life-scale toward societies (e.g., how Bill Gates saw himself as a philanthropist).

You can always see three dementions of outcomes when you consider your life- scale, and when you compare EXPERIENCE vs TIME:

1. **Learning:** Are you learning as you progress in your life?

2. **Valuable:** How valuable are you becoming?

3. **Responsibility:** As you are growing, do you take more responsibility?

Lets explore little more in to career-scale.

Career-Scale:

> *"All around the world, people want to escape the evils of boredom, vice, and need, and instead find mastery, autonomy, and purpose by working."*
>
> **– Brynjolfsson and McAfee,**
> ***The Second Machine Age* (2014)**

How do you define your career? A career is defined as very transactional and objective, and is a collection of work we do day-to-day. Most of us spend approximately 85,000 to 95,000 hours of our lives either at work or building our careers. So work should be considered as a crtitical issue in your day-to-day living and what it means to you and your family. I am sure it is not just "work," or a list of work that you do to get paid. It has more meaning—what you want out of your work, and what you become during your work, is more important than it just being "work." If you look up the word, *work*, in the dictionary, it would say something along the lines of, *"to do something for someone else for pay."* Oftentimes, synonyms for work include *daily struggle, grind,* and *drudgery*.It is on this notion that we have built our organizations for over the last 100 years. The work used to be one-sided. Organizations provided a job, and employees showed up to complete them. That is the reason we called it a very transactional and objective process to carry out the work. Now we are moving toward a world where work is about experience, exposure, expertise, relationship, and doing something with a sense of purpose. Work may be about doing something you want to do everyday, and being motivated, but not be drudgery. Organizations are requiring employee experience, and new technology is being proposed and promoted in the digital workplace. The focus is on creating corporate cultures and sustainable growth, but we need to explore how and why. I have written a complete chapter on career planning and setting up your goals to achieve.

Why are you working, and what is the purpose of your work in your daily life?

What does work mean to you, your family, and your career?

How does it relate and be relevent to the individual, family, and society at large?

What defines good, healthy, and worthwhile work?

What does money have to do with your job and career, and how important is it to you ?

What do experience, growth, and fulfillment have to do with jobs, careers, and your future-scale ?

Do you plan to create multiple talent skills or to stack big things in your life?

And most important question !

 "The most important question to ask on the job is not, 'What am I getting?' The most important question to ask is, 'What am I becoming?'"

– Jim Rohn

When you compare your **EXPERIENCE** vs **TIME,** you can always see three dementions of outcomes when you are considering your job, career, and growth, especially in today's global knowledge and digital era, where change is the only constant, and uncertainty becomes a daily routine.

1. **Learning:** Are you learning enough in your job and your daily life?

2. **Valuable:** How valuable are you becoming in your future job, personally and for growth?

3. **Responsibility:** Are you getting enough responsibility, and growing with responsibility, to become a future leader?

Lets explore more deeper in to your dream-scale.

Dream-Scale:

A dream is an imaginary series that you experience in your mind while you work on your life-scale and work-scale. A situation or event can be thought of as a dream if you often think about it, and you would like it to happen for you and your family.

As you can see, in the diagram below, you can have multiple work views in your career-scale, dream-scale, and life-scale. If you have a strong dream-scale, then everything in your job, work, and life will pull you toward your dream, which will give you the sucessful life you desire. This takes more time and many iterative cycles in order to achieve it. Each zone brings opportunities and challenges from which you get equal rewards.

2.2 LIFE-SCALE

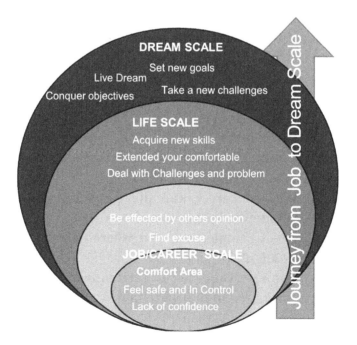

Limiting self-belief: My job and career are not well aligned with my dream.

Reality: To achieve the best from your job and career, you need to know what you are becoming while working. To make your life meaningful, you need to have a dream and a long-term vision in your career, and align yourself.

What you are becoming is an important question to ask yourself.

Your dream-scale is the integration and the outcome of your career-scale, work-scale, and life-scale. The bigger the dreams are that you can imagine for yourself, your family, society, and the world, the better the world will be for all of us. When you integrate your job and career with your dream-scale, you will find that it both complements and clashes, but you need to observe and fine-tune as you progress to better outcomes for your future.

The few questions to ask yourself:

What is your dream? And do you believe in your dream or in karma?

How is it aligned with your career-scale, work-scale and life-scale?

What kind of career and life do you dream for yourself and family, in the future?

How does it complement, and where does it clash? How does it align?

How do you get your energy and motivation to build your dream-scale, and to believe in it?

Next, we will discuss how you build the tools, method, and process that is required to set up the foundation to succeed in the future.

You can always refer to three-dimentional outcomes when you are considering your dream-scale, and when you are comparing experience vs time, in the short and long term:

1. **Family Values**: How well are you aligned with your job and career to fulfill long- term dreams?

2. **Freedom**: How free are you from any financial worry or liability? How are these relevant to your family, friends, and society?

3. **Responsibility**: Are you enjoying your responsibilities and making your life meaningful, and are you getting enough responsibility to enable you to grow in your personal, professional, and career development?

Quick Summary:

In plotting your future, it requires 3 dimensions: life-scale, career-scale, and dream-scale. By combining all three, you can achieve a meaningful, joyful, and successful life. Plotting is like searching and finding a direction to achieve your desired goal in each area of your life, and creating value in yourself.

Let's do some activities to get clarity before moving on.

EXPLORING ACTIVITY 2.1: PLOTTING YOUR FUTURE OF LIFE, CAREER, and WORK & DREAM SCALE

1. Write down your life-scale point regarding the following questions, and discuss it with your family and friends, and a mentor or coach, if you have one, based on **2.2 LIFE –SCALE**:

   - What is the meaning and purpose of life?

   - How is your relationship with your family and friends?

   - What is a good life-scale definition to you and your family?

   - What is your spiritual point of view? How does it affect you personally?

   - How does it affect your art and play in your life?

2. Write down and discuss your career-scale and work-scale, in at least 100 to 150 words, with a minimum of 5 key objectives and outcomes.

   - Why do you work, and what is the meaning of your work?

   - What does money have to do with work?

   - What do experience, growth, and fulfillment have to do with work?

   - What does work mean to you in the short and long term?

- How does it relate to you as an individual, to your family, and to society?

- What defines good, healthy, and worthwhile fitness?

3. Write down your dream-scale point and how it complements or clashes with your life-scale point, career-scale point, and work-scale point (in the short term and long term).

    - What is your dream? How is it aligned with your career-scale, work-scale, and life-scale?

    - How does it complement, and where does it clash?

    - What turns you on? How do you get your fuel and energy to motivate and build your dream-scale point?

(Note: Please think about and review this before you write about any view points and how they affect each other from a long-term perspective.)

Make sure you complete this before moving to the next chapter. If you don't write about it, you will forget. Writing has many benefits in the short and long term.

"Our greatest weakness lies in giving up. The most certain way to succeed is always to try just one more time."

—Thomas A. Edison

Constructing

Paul was an excellent student throughout his academic career in computer science, and completed his engineering program at one of the most prestigious engineering colleges in India. His parents were very proud of him, as he had been mentored and coached by both his mother and father. Paul's analytical skills and coding knowledge, in multiple domains, were exceptionally strong, with the best academic performance during his engineering degree. In his final year at his collage, during campus selection, he received 3 joint offers from Fortune 500, global MNCs, as a data scientist. A friend, in his inner circle, wanted to pursue (MBA) a master's in business administration (MBA), in the USA. Paul also finally received an offer from one of the top colleges in the USA, and he was convinced to pursue an MBA as well. He continued his master's in business, with a specialization in international marketing, but Paul liked his coding and analytical skills more; and he was not only passionate about but was also obsessed with programming languages, and computer language coding. During the day, he would do lots of research to learn about demand and supply, macro and micro economics, country trade policies, legal responsibilities, marketing strategies, search engine optimization (SEO) and social marketing, promotion and pricing, Michael Porter and BCG Consulting, etc.

At night, he was learning computer coding and new

artificial intelligence and analytical skills. He was progressing very well but very slowly, as it was difficult for him to balance both subjects and domains at the same time, and his performance was lower compared to his peers and friends. He was lacking structure, guidance, and focus, and was unable to decide whether to focus on his business management or on AI programming and coding.

 Limiting self-belief: If I don't get my higher education and business management degree, I will be left behind in my career growth.

Reality: The world is moving toward highly specialized and deep competency, but at the same time requires strong dual competency and focus on a talent stacking platform, due to shifting toward automation and artificial intelligence.

*The world is looking for humans who have the expertise to program AI/ML and robotic process automation. It's never too late to get a management degree. Focus on one skill at a time, become an expert in one area, and then develop alternative skills to lead toward dual deep competency.

Learn one deep competency at a time, but build the talent stacking platform.

Constructing Your Fundamentals

"If you don't build your dream, someone will hire you to help build theirs."

—**Tony Gaskins**

The construction of your future means laying down your foundation for success, by developing and building skills, and practicing on a regular basis. As we have talked about life, career, job, and dream-scales in the last chapter, we need to visualize each of the view points; and we need to construct and find the opportunity to be optimistic and to set your goals toward each, measuring the progress and fine-tuning as you progress, and when required, apply all the tools and processes. The interesting thing about constructing in today's world, in the Informaiton and digital machine era, is that all the information is available, and it will help you navigate and find an opportunity to network with others in the same industries, or with the same group of people who want to develop and support each other. But all this is dependent on what is called "self.x." The four fundamentals of constructing your future are self-confidence, self-discipline, self-reliance, and self-education, which makes us stronger and able to take any steps in life. "Self.x" is a factor, which shows that you are responsible for architecting your future, and for your own destiny. Unless you take responsibility, nothing will move toward you. Success attracts success, and you will attract it when you take responsibility on your own.

3.1 FOUR SELF-DEVELOPMENT APPROACHES

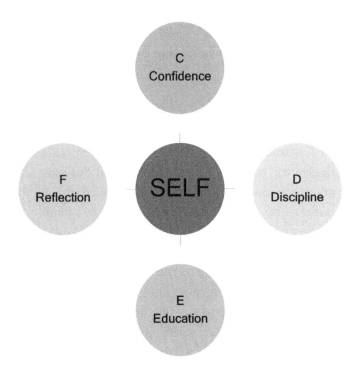

Self-confidence is the first step to starting your own journey in the digital economy; it plays a key role, as information is overflowing, and self-confidence helps you bring information closer to you, to make you successful. The good part is that self-confidence is behavioural science, and it alters and improves as you progress. Learn to apply and understand, and relearn and explore; take small steps, prototype it, implement it ,and confirm it.

Self-discipline is a major aspect if you really want to be a success. With self- discipline, you drive yourself with full motivation, which makes it easy to accomplish things. In order to construct and jump to the next step, we will need to do things that we normally don't like to do. However, those small steps are going to help you get to the next steps toward your goals and aspiring in your future. These are going to teach you to work hard and smart, even if you don't like it or enjoy it. Anyone can accomplish something extraordinary, but keeping in mind and having the strength to do the tedious work, is what is going to help you to reach your goal. You need to know that sometimes life is going to be difficult, and you also need to keep your mind positive. There will come a time when all of your hard work and sacrifices are going to pay off, and you just need to believe that it is going to happen. Through the constructing journey, you need to keep your mind on it, and align all your view points together to have success—know that you are one step closer to grabbing your dreams.

Self-education, when I was younger, was one of the most important things; I have learned the value of education and self-education. The ability to want to continue to re-invent yourself is an unquenchable desire. The skill is such a key characteristic, and it will assist you in your growth. If you want to get anywhere in life, then you will need to continue to learn a wide variety of things, which may not even pertain to your goal. I call this *vertical development*, and we will discuss it in detail. An important thing that I have learned is that it is valuable to have the mindset of exloring and wanting to learn. This extra couple of hours of giving your mind new challenges will benefit the architecting of your future. Becoming self-educated means that you need to want to learn new things, and to explore. The hunger to want to explore and learn is a fruitful characteristic, and is the foundation of constructing, which will benefit you for the rest of your life.

Self-reflection and reliance on yourself is a hard aspect to grasp. Life can be stressful at times, and that is why we learn to depend on other people for help and support. However, being self-reliant is an important skill and characteristic for individual success in the digital era. Today, we are fortunate that we are living in the greatest time in history, where we have so much information available at our fingertips for self-reliance and reflection, to construct our lives for a better future.

Although architecting your future and your life is almost vital for the workforce of the future, to have the capability of working with others, and building your inner-circle and outer-circle, it is also important to know how to do things on your own. Self-reliance requires self-discipline and self-reflection. Self-reliance is a step-by-step process, and it is pivotal to having the capability to be patient and self-confident, which you have to incorporate throughout your life. The key to being self-reliant is to trust yourself and be ready for the future. If you don't trust yourself to accomplish things, then it will be difficult to get anywhere in life, as no one else will trust you. It is important that the main person you rely on is yourself. You need to trust your decisions, and that you are making the right choices for you and your future. If you have trust in yourself that you are capable, and that you have the capability to lead your future, then succeeding in your life becomes easy.

Your Daily Performance and Enhancement Requires Vital Energy

Constructing your future is directly related to your performance, either daily, monthly, or annually, for your career, health, education, or family. Your performance is the driving force and motivation factor to help you move from your current state to your future state.

 Limiting self-belief: I am too busy with my work, and I don't have time to study new subjects or learn new skills.

Reality: To achieve your optimum performance, you need to be curious about learning. Emotion, fueled by positive physiology, gives you positive behavior, and positive behavior will provide optimum results. (growth mindset)

In order for you to achieve the desired result, you need to focus on your physiology, emotions, feelings, thinking, and behaviour. If you keep a positive physiology, and feed positive electromagnetic fields to your emotions, you will produce positive emotions. Emotion is an electromagnetic motion in your body, and it is either positive (+ve) or negative (-ve). If you feed your emotions with positive things, you will get a positive feeling, and when you have positive feelings, then it brings positive thinking. With positive thinking, you bring positive behaviour, and you produce positive results. That way, you can keep your performance consistent, and achieve optimum results in your life. The important factor for your performance is your *E-motion*: Electromagnetic motion. If you can control your emotions, you can change your life. Always try to keep moving toward positive emotions.

There are 34,000 emotions, and there are 12 to 14 that we use most of the time. Your emotions will predict your behavior, your success, and your life. If you want to be successful, you need to control your emotions in order to make the right decisions. This concept is explained in a fishbone diagram format so that it is easily understood.

3.2 PHYSIOLOGY AND EMOTION LEADS TO PERFORMANCE

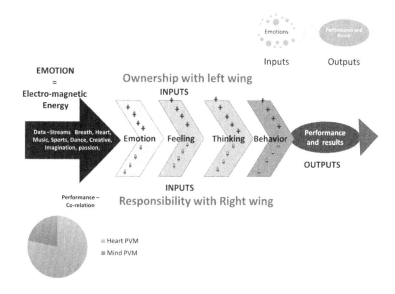

As you can see in the above diagram, physiology consists of all the streams of signals that could be positive or negative, based on our mental and physical activities that are considered sources of energy, and which produce the highest performance and significant results through behaviors.

But the question arises whether you would maintain the momentum of positive emotional flow in daily life. Let's understand *the momentum*.

Your Momentum

Momentum and flow play a key role in constructing and maintaining perfomance. Once you understand performance enhancers and your emotions—which I call "energy in motion"—with energy linked with performance, you may need to maintain the momentum of your thoughts and feelings, and be required to rejuvinate whenever you feel unbalanced or negative, so that you can push your energy to go one step higher.

3.3 MOMENTUM P-E OWNERSHIP GRAPHS:
P-E Ownership (Physiology-Emotion Graphs)

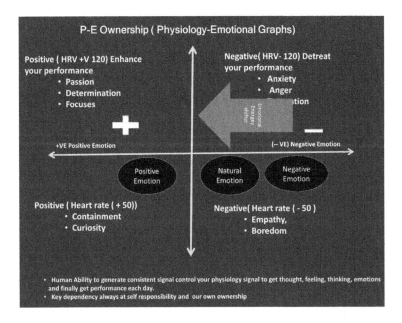

We live with uncertainty and fear, so in order to maintain our momentum, we need to bring passion, determination, focus, self-awareness, and positivity through, to bring change in our mindset, and to drive positivity into our daily lives. This is also directly linked with your inner circle—your family, kids, and positive associations.

Dr. Atkin talks about coherence and your ability to generate coherent signals in your heart and mind by controling your physiology signals to get thoughts, feelings, and emotions, and to finally get performance every day. The key to dependency will be responsibility and ownership of your momentum, to be positive and manage your heart's variable rate through mindfulness.

Why Anticipation, Observation, and Predicting is Important

Anticipation, observation, and dreaming is key to architecting your future. Today's and tomorrow's technology will continue to impact our lives. Our workers, at every level in today's ever-changing labor market, need to be prepared with skills to adapt and succeed in their workplaces, careers, and lives.

Limiting self-belief: Technology is changing so fast that we can't keep up with skills in the next digital era.

Reality: If you have followed the trends and have been observing anticipatory careers, you can predict your future and which direction your life or career is heading. Technology trends are key to seeing your progress.

It is a problem as well as an opportunity to live in an uncertain, complex, and fast moving innovative world, and because of the high levels of uncertainty that we all face, people of all ages and career levels are finding it difficult to know what new skills to adopt and learn, what courses to take, and what degree/certification to get that will provide them with the most opportunity going forward. Uncertainty keeps us stuck in the present situation. Certainty, on the other hand, gives us the opportunity and confidence to make a bold decision, to move forward with confidence, and to invest time, money, and energy to learn new and more things. Over the past twenty years, I have been working and have developed a proven architecture methodology to anticipate what leads to disruption, and practice to change it before it happens, which allows you to find the confidence that will provide certainty. This is a new science of certainty, which involves and requires a scientific method of separating remaining trends and trends that will happen in the future, from soft trends—trends that might happen.

This method is currently being applied and used by many individuals and many mulitnational organizations globally, for which I have worked and experienced. It provides an accurate roadmap of the opportunities that are ahead, based on my technology trends, customer consulting, industry solutions, and management and sales experience.

You are very special. That's why this book in your hand is called *Architecting Your Future,* and is supported by architecting and architectural thinking. And it is why I'm now helping you to connect the dots on how the 7 new technology trends will help you drive and transform your career, and create new opportunities for you. By providing an accurate roadmap for anyone who wishes to increase their personal career relevancy, in a world of changing technological and transformative skills, I can help you make your career and educational decisions, with confidence, for the future.

The list highlights technologies that are now transforming, and will continue to transform, present and future careers. As you read through the list, ask yourself how each one will play a key role in your industry and your personal career path, and make you successful.

"If you see a future, and you have a promising future, you will invest, and you will go on and on to make it happen."

—Ravindar Kumar

Importance of Goals

Your Goals Determine Your Future

Construction, enhancement, momentum,and anticipation are definitely strong requirements for architecting your future—but not without a goal. The type of goal and size of goal will determine the direction and destination of your future, and will also drive you to go the extra mile, even during the tough times in your life.

> *"The trouble with not having a goal is that you can spend your life running up and down the field and never score."*
>
> —Bill Copeland

So, if you can see and have a promising future, you will invest, and you will go on and on.

Many people today are struggling through life. Even though they work hard, they don't feel like they are getting what they want. That is because they are not building a system, and they are not giving enough importance to goals; they do not have a direction in which to go, for what they want to achieve. I have interviewed hundreds of students and graduates, and they are not sure what to do with their lives, or which direction to choose. There are even many professional adults who work for years and are surprised when they reach middle-age and don't know what to do next, and they felt stuck in their life's journey.

When you give less importance to your goals, and you

stop setting goals and thinking about what you want, you break out of auto-pilot, and you start living a life of your own conscious mind direction. Instead of letting other people tell you what to do, you proactively take charge and think about what you want for yourself to get maximum results. High-performing business professionals, world IT leaders, world-class athletes, and other successful people all set goals, and they take them seriously. Michael Phelps (competitive swimmer and most decorated Olympian of all time), Sachin Tendulkar (former India international cricket captain, and highest run scorer and greatest batsman of all time in international cricket), Kobe Bryant (NBA star), Richard Branson (business magnate), and Elon Musk (CEO of SpaceX and Tesla Motors) all set goals. That is because when you set goals, you have a vision to work toward, and you push yourself to get the best results; and you make things happen rather than resting and waiting for things to happen. We all know what gets measured and what gets improved, and you can see the results. If you don't set specific targets and milestones, how will you architect your future? When I architect a system for an enterprise, the first thing to know is the end-goal, and then to work backward to achieve the goal by each and every milestone, accomplishing it in a timely manner. As the popular saying goes, *"Shoot for the moon. Even if you miss, you will land among the stars."* When you set goals and understand the importance of why you are doing it, you're aiming for the moon. Your goals propel you to take more action than you would have otherwise. Know that all things are created twice: first in the mind, and then in the physical world. The mental creation happens when you set goals. The physical creation happens when you work on your goals with actions and milestones. Without mental creation, the physical creation can't happen. Goals also give you laser focus as to what and where exactly you should spend your positive energy and time, to get going in your life, daily and for the long term.

This is a true way that technologists approach any real problem. Let's say that you set a goal to become chief digital officer (CDO) for a large IT company, as everyone today wants digital transformation. Even though you have no idea how to become a CDO, the very act of setting a goal gives you focal points and a curious mind. As you understand the role of CDO, and you brainstorm for ideas, you will realize that you can start by studying the market and how you can convert your marketing products and skills to apply the digital media, so that you can reach a maximum audience and master your skills. At the same time, you can test your product and let your friends sample your creation, either on social media or via an application, before launching it globally. By following this, and analyzing, you will be able to master and achieve your goal.

YOUR CIRCLE OF INFLUENCE, PURSUASION, AND ASSOCIATION

Never underestimate the power of influence and influencers. Peer pressure is a powerful influencer for life. Learning through the association of influencers is always the best option to architecting your life. For example, people around you most likely don't read books, so you will not read a book. Most of the time, your parents always advised you that you should only play with kids that had good behavior, and to follow the obedient friends who have higher goals and a purpose in life. Sometimes you loved to play with those kind of friends, and it would really pay off in your future. Today, life is more fun and socially connected, due to digital, social associations and social media.

In regard to your inner circle of influencers, persuasion, and associations.

There are four key questions to ask yourself:

a) **Who do I hang around with?**

b) **What am I feeding my mind?**

c) **What effect are they having on me? What kind of mindset am I building? What are they making me read? What are they making me listen to?**

d) **Is it okay? Be either positive or negative, but observe your inner voice.**

Look at the outcomes and objective, and analyze it for yourself.

Key Notes:

Everything matters, and ignorance is never the best policy. Knowing is the best policy, and awareness is important in order to discuss and decide what your next steps will be. And, I want to know what the effect on my life is.

It's easy to let people influence you, but you have to keep on checking. Either you are getting positively influenced or negatively influenced, then you have to act accordingly—the choice is yours.

You are the architect of your future, and you may have to make some hard choices for a better future:

Choice #1 – Associations: Be disciplined and associate with successful, positive people to have accomplishments.

Keep asking yourself who you can associate with to make positive changes. You don't have to be wealthy to start with; you just need to be smart and to start the right plan. Find someone that is healthy, and start your health plan with them. Sometimes it's important to spend some money in order to spend time with successful people, and to get smart tips—get your plan from successful people. Plot a scheme to do whatever you have to do, but **just do it**. Find a successful person to start your success and lifestyle plan.

I call it **"Association on Purpose."** Associate with the right people to make and guide you to be successful—increase your successful circle of influencers. I always find the best person to influence me and direct me to go in the right direction, and who has the ability to observe and remember in detail.

Choice #2 –Limited associations: If you are spending major time on minor things, the best policy is to spend major time with major associations, and minor time with minor associations. Look at how your time is spent on priorities. It's okay to have casual friends that you spend casual time with, but not serious time. For example, you can spend 20% on minor time, and 80% on major time; or 30% on minor, and 70% on major—but not the opposite.

Choice #3 – Dissociation: This is the need to discard or remove negative associations in your life, which are toxic for your success in life. If you are not thinking about and giving importance to your associations, it can be a disaster in the long term.

There are bigger questions to ask, for your career development and planning.

Where do you go for intellectual influence?

You need to associate with successful people so that you can learn from them and be successful.

Ideas are highly influenced by education; education is influenced by people, and people influence people.

Check and measure your progress. The basic rule of success is that if you can't measure it, you can't improve.

What about health goals?

Investment goals?

Travel goals?

Friendship goals?

Happiness goals?

Social support goals?

Family goals?

Share with others that you meet. Read a book, possibly write a book, educate your children, explore Rome… learn something new, and become a social entrepreneur to impact society and look forward.

Method:

The architecting method is a proven, step-by-step process that works; it is a system to define your vision and goals, and help you follow through to define your success path. This is called the *integrated career development method.* It's called this because it is aligned with your career requirements, career vision, and bigger dreams, and there is a lot of iteration throughout, as the future is unknown, and it changes as it progresses. In this journey, a lot of tools, processes, and framework is required in order to be successful. Once you apply these, then you can replicate them the next time, to get expedited solutions, outcomes, and results.

This model is also aligned with the ICT framework from

the development, learning, enablement, and growth phases of success.

3.4 UEDIC MODEL (Understand, Explore, Develop, Implement, and Confirm):

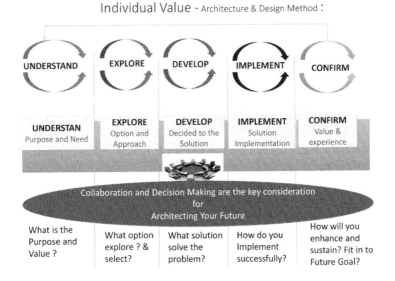

Individual Value - Architecture & Design Method :

UNDERSTAN Purpose and Need	EXPLORE Option and Approach	DEVELOP Decided to the Solution	IMPLEMENT Solution Implementation	CONFIRM Value & experience

Collaboration and Decision Making are the key consideration for Architecting Your Future

What is the Purpose and Value ?	What option explore ? & select?	What solution solve the problem?	How do you Implement successfully?	How will you enhance and sustain? Fit in to Future Goal?

Integrated Career Development Method

I know it looks like a complex diagram, but it is simple to understand. Its integrated career development methodology is pictorial, representing career development, starting from a long-term career vision, and following through with a career goal. It focuses on specializing in information communication technology (ICT) as a career prospective, with deeper, specialized jobs in network and communication, starting with technical engineering and growing toward the leadership path. To achieve better results in life, every individual has to go through various stages of learning, struggling, and having a willingness to dedicate themselves. It requires clear, deep thinking, from the development to the enabling stage, to finally achieve the growth stage. Some time is required in this multiple iteration process, to do it again and again, to become a master in your domain.

3.5 Architecting Your Future – ICT Method:

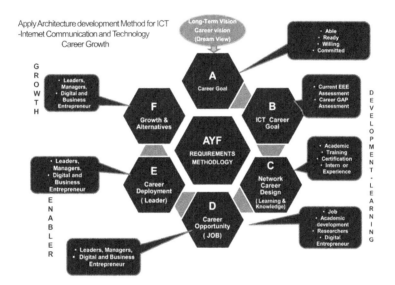

A similar integrated method has been adopted by many Fortune 100 companies to define their organization's architecting, to design their product, project, and organization, to achieve their optimum results.

These are simple steps, but each step requires the exploring of deeper skills to learn and understand.

3.6 FOUR STEPS TO GROWTH

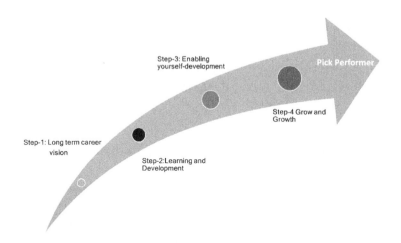

    The four integrated steps process is aligned by a long-term career vision and goal. The pragmatic approach is aligned with development, learning, enablement, and growth.

    Let's go step-by-step to explore learning.

    Step 1: A long-term career vision starts out in the development phase, as a long- term strategic assessment of your dream view point is required of your career goals. You may have multiple career goals, so you may need to align your career goals with career visions.

    Step 2: Learning and development is about selecting your career goal and working towards a) career goal b) ICT career goal c) network career design; d) career/job opportunity. This helps you to start a strong foundation, and helps you to get strong growth to align with your career vision.

    Step 3: Enabling your self-development is the leadership development of your career plan, which helps you to grow in the same ICT career; or if you decide to choose an alternative, you can choose to prepare for an alternative growth plan.

Step 4: Growth is the path toward **dual deep competency**, and it helps you build your system to define your multiple career goals, to align with your career vision.

To support your growth from step one to step four, you need to have strong desires, faster and curious learning, and an adaption mechanism. In today's digital era, speed matters most—those who learn faster, will be leaders for the future.

Limiting self-belief: I am doing very well in my life and may need to work hard to learn new skills.

Reality: You cannot do well in your life if you are no longer able to manage your learning skills and competency in the digital era.

FAST AND CURIOUS—"LEARN FAST, LEARN MORE, AND BE A LEADER."

Speed matters in the digital era. The **fast and curious** is a process to approach any learning and to step-up any subject, or to re-skill in a very moderate amount of time, to develop to a professional level. Traditionally, if you wanted to become an expert performer or a world-class champion, then you would need to apply the 10,000-hour rule. This practice rule used to be true in the past, but to start with, if you want to be a professional associate, you just need 20 hours of dedicated prototyping time to reach and become an optimum performer. Once you have created an interest, and you know it is well-aligned with your career and dream-scale, then you can choose the path of an expert. The graph below shows how you can keep your short-term learning approach to become a long-term, world-class expert.

3.7 FOUR STEPS FOR FAST AND CURIOUS LEARNING

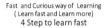

Fast and Curious way of Learning
(Learn fast and Learn more)
4 Step to learn fast

 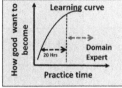

4 steps to Fast and Curious learning any subject and Domain:
Step-1 Deconstruct the skills to be Ready to Learn .
Step-2 Learn enough to self-correct with limited time to have overview
Step-3 Remove Practice barriers to skill up .
Step-4 Practice at least -20 Hours to spend learn the subject or develop the skills architecting think method.

Note : 10,000 hours practice required to become , master, expert and champion to learn for sport, chess, or athletic and area
The Major barrier to skills acquisition is not intellectual..... It s emotional.
Research shown to become Expert Skilled Champion :
Spend 10,000 hours to acquired skills and Become a Domain Expert

The major barrier to skills acquisition is not intellectual—it's emotional.

To have expert skills and become a champion, you have to spend 10,000 hours to be an authority on a single subject.

Practice makes you better; deliberate practice makes you a master. When you are learning something with curiosity, and you want to be good, you measure how good you are and how fast you pick up the knowledge and skill to be a legend.

Apply the process below, and you will see the radical results and improvement in yourself.

Step-1 Deconstruct the skills: Decide exactly what you want to learn, and break it down into small parts to learn it.

Step-2 Learn enough to self-correct: Get 3 to 5 different sources to learn and practice from (books, DVDs, articles, YouTube videos, seminars, your inner-circle, etc.)

Step-3 Remove practice barriers: Avoid distractions, such as TV, social media, negative talk, fears, and worries.

Step-4 Focus and spend 20 hours to learn the subject: You could spend 45 minutes a day, for a month. Spend at least 20 hours on each skill, and commit to focus for this amount of time. With this approach, you will become a fast and life-long learner, and a high performer in any area to achieve extraordinary results. I call it **"learning fast and learning more to be a leader."** You have to learn more than what you need, and be ahead of others in the digital era.

3.8 HIGH PERFORMER LEARNING CYCLE:

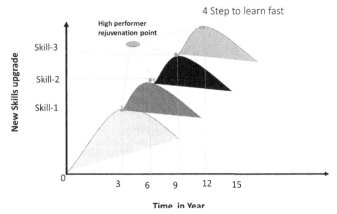

Life cycle of high performance Learner

How to build and maintain high performer learning skills cycle:

Today, technology is moving so fast in every industry, and you need to continue to have a learning and adaptive skills mindset. You also need to acquire new skills every 3 to 5 years. Keeping your performance and skills up-to-date helps you to be a performer in each industry.

This is a high performer learning life-scale to build the multiple skills you need in order to perform in your daily life. But how can you continue to upgrade your skills in today's digital economy and high flowing information highway?

Whatever skills and knowledge you develop, get obsolete and outdated within 2 to 3 years. To keep up, you have to continue to learn fast and learn more, and continue learning and re-inventing yourself every 3 years, to rejuvenate with building **dual deep competency**. If you keep learning 1 or

2 skills every 3 years of the cycle, you will maintain your competency and learning curve as a high-class performer.

I was interviewing a very senior doctor from Singapore hospital, who had been practicing medicine for the last 25 years. His profession requires extensive skills development. I asked him how he was able to keep up his skills in medicine, and how he compared himself to someone who was just getting their doctorate degree in medicine, as well as who would become his competitor.

His answer surprised me—he applied the same 20-hour rule to learn quickly and develop more skills, and to keep his skills and knowledge up to date in his area, as well as knowing what is happening in other parts of the world. He was keeping his long-term career vision to adopt cognitive learning skills and develop double deep competency strategies, with 10,000 hours of deliberate practice to maintain his expert and legendary level.

Even this strategy has been adopted and applied by many global, multinational companies to develop their new products' lifecycle and life-scale, to reinvent themselves every 2 to 3 years, to be competitive in the market and be industry leaders.

This is how people end up loving what they do for a living.

I always ask myself this question:

Why do people love their work?

These are the answers I get:

- **Creativity: learning new things**

- **Control: when what you do makes you proud**

- **Impact: positive influence of your work and impact on others**

3.9 RARE AND VALUABLE SKILLS:

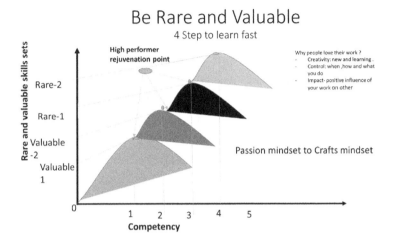

How do people end up loving what they do for a living ?
DID NOT follow their passion ..

To keep on learning, you need to acquire updated skills every 3 to 5 years, and to create a craft mindset. But more importantly, you need to become rare and valuable, so you need to develop rare and valuable skills in order to be the best performer in your industry. To command the position of a world-class expert, and to become a legend, you require a flowing mindset:

1. Create a craft mindset rather than a passion mindset, where you are always willing to protect, defend, and attack new challenges, and to create multiple skills before reaching your peak.

2. Take on challenging projects, and keep learning beyond paycheck and money.

3. The following steps of daily deliberate practice will help you become a legend:

    A. Have periods of undistracted focus.

    B. Shift back and forth from comfort to discomfort.

    C. Get immediate feedback and expert guidance, and be willing to re-invent yourself as you progress.

Quick Summary

In constructing your future chapter, we have started with the 4 fundamentals (your self-CDEF strategy): self-confidence, self-discipline, self-education, and self-reliance, and reflection is the first step. To make your life more productive, emotions linked with performance, physiology, and electromagnetics, which I call "E-motion," is the source and input of positive thinking, feeling, and behavior, to shape your daily life-scale. There is too much negativity and ambiguity around us, which keeps us from achieving our goals and enjoying our daily lives. To keep the momentum and flow is the source of daily sustainability. Our energy links with performance, either negative or positive, depending on how we think, feel, behave, and act. And the good part is that it can change and improve. We have also discussed anticipation and observation, to keep track of trends so that we can architect our future, but this is never possible without goals. If you are considering setting a goal, without giving importance to identifying your purpose, and without a circle of influence, it will be hard to achieve. So, every aspect is important in consideration of constructing your future. Architecting your future requires a long-term strategy, mindset, and methodology. I have created the UEDIC MODEL (understand, explore, develop, implement, and confirm), which you can build and replicate for as many careers as you want. The beauty of this model is that it has been taken from the architectural thinking of successful methodology that we apply in the real world of information and communication technology. It has been defined and based on understanding, exploring multiple options, developing and sticking with one thing at a time, and implementing and confirming to move on to the next. Being a curious and fast learner, and adapting and learning more and more knowledge in our economy, will be a key principle for success. Finally, learn how to be in demand, as rare skills are valuable to architecting your future.

TO BE A CONTINUED SUCCESS
IN THE DIGITAL ERA,
GOALS, SYSTEMS, AND FOCUS PLAY
A VITAL ROLE FOR ARCHITECTURING
YOU FUTURE.

EXPLORING ACTIVITY 3.1: CONSTRUCTING YOUR ENERGY AND PERFORMANCE

1. What keeps you up late at night? Researching on the internet to keep up your skills?

2. What motivates you every day, and what kind of goal do you define for yourself?

3. How do you feel and think about your job every day, and about your workout, exercise, and everyday goals?

4. Do you have a self-CDEF strategy to keep up your life, career, and dream-scales? Write down your 4 CDEF.

5. Who is your inner-circle of influence and association, and how frequently do you communicate with your like-minded friends? How often are you in touch with your inner-circle of influence? Do you see any impact on yourself?

6. What is your UEDIC (understand, explore, develop, implement and confirm) plan for your career? Identify 2 to 3 key skills that can help you be rare and unique in your field and continue developing.

"The best way to predict the future is to create it."

— **Abraham Lincoln**

Promises of Goals

Goals, Systems, and Focus

Your goals, system, and focus is like a three-dimensional viewpoint, and we need all three sides of the viewpoint to be balanced to get real experience and optimum results. We need all sides to be equally valuable. Sometimes setting goals alone is not the only problem that you face. Another time, choosing the right goals, without a system to begin with, is the hardest way to see the progress.

Basically, you can choose to work on any goal that you feel is necessary for your health, economics, financial stability, and happiness. Goal setting is nothing more than a formal process for personal planning, and a process for execution of a system. By setting goals on a routine basis, you decide what you want to achieve and how, and then you move in a step-by-step manner toward the achievement of these goals.

The process of setting goals and targets allows you to choose where you want to go in life. By knowing exactly what you want to achieve, you will know what action you have to concentrate on to do it. You will also know when something is nothing more than a distraction.

> **Limiting self-belief:** I set my goal, and I will achieve it.
>
> **Reality:** Setting the goal is only one step of the overall process, and you need to build the system in order to succeed in your goals, and continue with consistent focus.

Build the system, not the goal.

Goal setting is a standard technique used by many professional athletes, successful business people, and high achievers in all fields. It gives you long-term vision and provides you with short-term motivation, and it requires the dedication of each block to have its own characteristic, priority, and role to play in your life.

It helps to focus your attention and knowledge, which helps you to organize your resources. By setting sharp and clearly defined goals, you can measure and take pride in the achievement of those goals. You can see progress in what might previously have seemed a long, pointless effort.

By setting goals, you will also raise your self-confidence, as you recognize your ability to meet the goals that you have set. The process of achieving goals, and seeing this achievement, gives you the confidence that you will be able to achieve higher and more difficult goals later on.

Goals are set on a number of different levels.

In the first place, you decide the purpose goal and objective, what you want to do with your life, and what the large-scale goals are that you want to achieve. I call this the *radical goal*. The goal should be big enough to drive you.

Second, you break these down into smaller parts so that you can reach your overall goals.

Finally, once you have your plan, you start working step-by-step and inch-by-inch toward achieving it, and you take actions to move forward.

Beginning your goal setting plans:

The best way to begin your goal is to remember, as Benjamin Franklin supposedly once said, *"If you fail to plan, you are planning to fail."* This section explains how to set personal and professional goals. It starts with your key objective and clear purpose goals, and then works through a series of lower level plans, culminating in a daily, weekly, and monthly to-do list. It then moves on to your life-scale and long-term goals.

By setting up this structure of plans, you can even break the biggest life goal down into a number of small tasks that you need to do each day to reach the long- term and lifelong goals.

The first step in setting personal goals is to consider what you want to achieve in your life, as setting lifetime goals gives you the overall perspective that shapes all other aspects of your decision making process and support system.

This helps you to have a broader and balanced coverage of all important areas in your life. Try to set goals in some or all of the following categories, in specific block models to block your priorities and follow through on your progress by sequence or parallel. There is no sequence required or any best way to do this; it depends on your choice, but you have enormous opportunities to go on and on. These are presented in the diagram below. Goal setting is your choice, and the more brutally honest you are, the better results you will get.

4.0 GOALS ARE A CHOICE

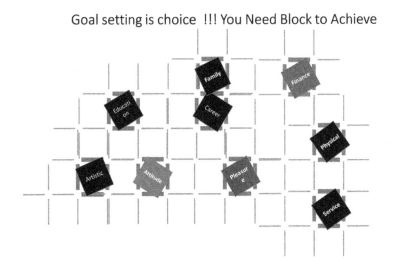

The above example gives you kinds of goals you can choose, and you can dedicate to build and set up a system to achieve the goal in your life. You can choose from any sequence or block to achieve it at any time in your life, based on your priorities, as you are the architect of your life and your future. I have given some examples of goals, but your goal can't be limited. Some examples of goals are:

- **Artistic:**

Do you want to achieve any artistic goals? If so, what is it? Do you want to write a book, paint a masterpiece, or compose a song?

- **Attitude:**

Does your own mindset hold you back from making progress? Is there any part of the way that you behave that upsets you—for example, do you talk too much? If so, set a goal to improve your behavior, or find a solution to the problem.

- **Career:**

What level do you want to reach in your career? Is it your goal to be the boss or own your own company someday, or do you want to be the president of someone else's company?

- **Education:**

Is there any knowledge you want to acquire in particular, or some area of study that you would like to pursue? What information and skills will you need to achieve these goals?

- **Family:**

Do you want to be a parent? If so, how are you going to be a good parent? How do you want your partner or family members to see you?

- **Financial:**

How much do you want to earn, by what age in your life? What can you do to make that come about?

- **Physical:**

Are there any athletic goals you want to achieve, or do you want good health deep into old age? What steps are you going to take to achieve this?

- **Pleasure:**

How do you want to enjoy yourself? You should ensure that some of your life is geared toward making yourself happy for no reason other than being happy.

- **Service:**

Do you want to make the world a better place by your existence? If so, how? Once you have decided your goals in these categories, you have to assign a priority to them if you want to succeed.

 "The best way to find yourself is to lose yourself in the services of others."

—**Mahatma Gandhi**

Then review the goals and re-prioritize until you are satisfied that they reflect the shape of the life that you want to lead. Also, you should ensure that the goals that you have set are the goals that you want to achieve, and not what your parents, spouse, family, or employers want them to be. Success only happens when you are working for your own wellbeing, because doing it for others will ensure that you sabotage your own success.

How to begin to achieve your goals:

"Know that you can start late, look different, be uncertain, and still succeed."

—Misty Copeland

Once you have set your long-term goals, the best thing that you can do is set a 10-year plan of smaller goals, which you should complete if you are to reach your long-term plan. From there, you can just shorten your overall goal spans. For example, you can set a 5-year plan, a 1-year plan, a 6-month plan, a 3-month plan, and a 1-month plan, of progressively smaller goals that you should reach to achieve your lifetime goals. Each of these should be based on the previous plan. It is the best way to begin to achieve a lifetime that is filled with results, without any failed wishes. It results in a life without regret. You see, by starting out slowly, you are giving yourself the chance to realize and work on achieving the goals that you set out to achieve. Nobody ever succeeds at attaining a goal that was forced. Those that tried never really got what they were hoping for. In rushing through and trying to achieve your goals quickly, you will likely miss a few key aspects that can really change your life's outcome. Think of it this way; if you were to run a full marathon, and decided to take a cab for half of the journey, have you really achieved that goal? Would you be satisfied when you crossed the finish line? It would be a hollow victory that could only provide a moment's happiness but not make you satisfied.

First, set a daily to-do list of the things that you should

do today and that matter most, to work toward and align your short-term and long-term goals. For example, at an early stage, these goals may be to read books and gather information on the achievement of your goals. This will help you to improve the quality and realism of your goal setting, and in effect, make it easier to achieve them. You also have to review your plans, and make sure that they fit the way in which you want to live your life. Once you have decided what your first set of plans will be, keep the process going by reviewing and updating your to-do list on a daily and weekly basis. You have to periodically review the longer-term plans, and change them to reflect your changing priorities and experiences in your life. I make my 52-week plan (1 year), and I divide it into 13-week sections. This way, I will have 4 big goals, and I will keep track of each 3-month plan so that I will get 4 outcomes every 3 months...

IS YOUR GOAL SETTING EFFECTIVE

There is a difference in setting your goals and setting them effectively. Anyone can set a goal, but doing it effectively means that it will actually get done.

There are so many things that you can do to better your life, but if you don't know how to go about it, you are stuck.

The following guidelines will help you to set effective goals and help you manage your time in an efficient manner that will cause those goals to become reality.

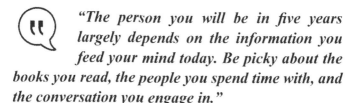

"The person you will be in five years largely depends on the information you feed your mind today. Be picky about the books you read, the people you spend time with, and the conversation you engage in."

—**Ruben Chavez**

The best goal setting approach, recommended by John Doerr, is to "measure what matters most in your life," by applying OKRs.

OKRs should be aligned with CFR (continuous feedback recognition). Objectives and key results matter for your professional and personal life, being in alignment with CFR. CFR is *continuous feedback recognition*, which is regular feedback aligned with your clear objective.

Simple example: My key objective is to run a full marathon. My key result would be to complete it on time.

CFR is like the measurement of every 5, 10, 20, 30, and finally 42.19 km target, and how you refine and maintain your momentum in every equal interval to support each step.

The **objective** is WHAT you want to achieve.

The **key result** is HOW you are going to achieve your objective by 3 to 5 clear and concise measurements, so that you are progressing and moving toward your short-term and long-term goals. The key results may include your growth, business revenue, and higher margin, adding new qualifications or professional certifications in order to be ahead of others, or even improving quality for customers to differentiate from others, or keeping a customer satisfaction score board, etc.

OKRs recommend 3 essentials:

- An **audacious objective** is the most interesting to start with—by being idealistic, not realistic. First, ask yourself: If you were free from constraints, what changes would you want to see in the world? And second, if you had an opportunity to be unique at one thing, what would that one thing be? After discovering a goal that inspires and motivates you, scale it back until it's one step short of being impossible. Your objective must be significant and inspiring, but believable so that you can keep pushing yourself harder with your inner spirit. When you believe in something realistically, you can achieve it easily, as you apply your positive emotion to achieve it.

A great and inspiring example is when Bill and Melinda Gates started the Gates Foundation. They set an *audacious* objective of eradicating malaria, by 2015. However, they realized that it was an impossible goal, which demotivated the team, so they adjusted their objective to eradicate malaria by 2040. The new objective was still big, but now it was believable. The audacious objective should inspire you and your team to grow to meet the challenge.

"When you try to do something BIG, you never entirely fail."

—**Larry Page**

- **Quality and quantity key results** are a strong set of key results, and specific measures of quality and quantity are the tools to target. When you keep quality and quantity as key results, you always try to work on reducing costly errors and re-work. At the same time, key results are like gauges on your car's dashboard. You want to increase the average speed while keeping your RPM meter and engine temperature low, so that you can get to your destination as efficiently as possible.

John Doerr explains: *"Objectives are the stuff of inspiration and far horizons. Key results are more earthbound and metric-driven."*

Color-coding check-ins are your tools for observation, improvement, and taking action. My mentor calls it "vision and action." The regular color-coding checks-ins will always remind you of your accountability for setting up challenging key result targets, making progress, and fine-tuning those key results, each week, month, quarter, or year (you choose the timeline based on your key results). Keep your observation on key results, and label each result as GREEN, YELLOW, or RED.

o Green indicates that you are 70% to 100% on your target, and you should continue with your current strategy.

o Yellow indicates that you are 30% to 70% on your target; you need a recovery plan, and you need to adjust your initial plan.

o Red indicates that you are 0% to 30% on your target, and you need to develop a recovery plan or replace the key results.

If you think there is no progress, and you are not having any improvement, then there is no need to stubbornly hold on to a goal or to outdated projections—strike it from your goal list, and move on. A nice way to say it is that our goals are our servants to our objectives and purpose, not the other way around.

"The biggest WARNING: If you are approaching 100% on all your key results, you have failed too. Aim for a mix of yellow and green key results, with an average key result score of 70% of your target. The biggest risk of all is not taking one."

—Mellody Hobson

STATE EACH GOAL AS A POSITIVE SPARK

Express your goals in a positive way. That is a key component to setting goals that you can attain. How often have you been excited to accomplish a goal that didn't even sound good when you brought it up? If you are not comfortable or happy with the goals that you have set, the likelihood of you succeeding is pretty low.

Limiting self-belief: I don't have visibility to set my goal for 5 years.

Reality: In today's digital era, short-term and long-term goals are equally important. Your goal setting is a first step to dreaming big for your life; it can define how successful you will be in your future.

Goals lead to success.

If you want to express your goals in a positive way, you simply have to first think of a goal that puts a smile on your face when you imagine it completed. Why would you want to set a goal that made you frown, cringe, or cry?

When you are beginning to set your goals, it helps when you are talking about them with others, in a manner that states your actions as positives, because it will have others seeing it as a positive as well. That will garner you a great deal more support. In the end, don't we all need a little support when we are trying to do something positive in our lives?

BE PRECISE

Set a precise goal that includes starting dates, times, and amounts so that you can properly measure your achievement. If you do this, you will know exactly when you have achieved the goal, and you can take complete satisfaction from having achieved it. Being precise in setting your goals is no more than setting them with exact details. It is easier this way because then you can follow a step-by-step format. That's all there is to it.

SET PRIORITIES

When you have several goals, give each a specific priority. This helps you to avoid feeling overwhelmed by too many goals, and helps to direct your attention to the most important ones and follow each in succession. Setting priorities will force you into the step-by-step format above. By doing the most important first, and moving to the least important in succession, you are enabling each task to be easier than the last. It causes the accomplishment of each task to get easier and easier, which will encourage you to complete your goal.

WRITE THE GOAL DOWN

This crystallizes your goals and gives them more force. In writing your goals down, you are better able to keep up with your scheduled tasks for each accomplishment. It also helps you to remember each task that needs to be done, and allows you to check them off as they are accomplished. Basically, you can better keep track of what you are doing so as not to repeat yourself unnecessarily.

KEEP OPERATIONAL GOALS SMALL

Keep the low-level goals that you are working toward, small and easy to achieve. If a goal is too large, then it can seem that you are not making progress. Keeping goals small and incremental allows you more opportunities for reward. Derive today's goals from larger ones. It is a great way to accomplish your goals.

SET PERFORMANCE GOALS, NOT OUTCOME GOALS

You should take care to set goals over which you have as much control as possible. There is nothing more dispiriting than failing to achieve a personal goal for reasons that are beyond your control. These could be bad business environments, poor judging, bad weather, injury, or just plain bad luck. If you base your goals on personal performance, then you can keep control over the achievement of your goals, and get satisfaction from achieving them.

SET REALISTIC GOALS

It is important to set goals that you can achieve. All sorts of people (parents, media, and society) can set unrealistic goals for you, which is almost a guarantee of failure. They will often do this in ignorance of your own desires and ambitions or flat out disinterest.

Alternatively, you may be naïve in setting very high goals. You might not appreciate the obstacles in the way, or not quite understand how many skills you must master to achieve a particular level of performance. By being realistic you are increasing your chances of success.

DO NOT SET GOALS TOO LOW

Just as it is important not to set goals unrealistically high, do not set them too low. People tend to do this where they are afraid of failure or where they simply don't want to do anything. You should set goals so that they are slightly out of your immediate grasp, but not so far that there is no hope of achieving them. No one will put serious effort into achieving a goal that they believe is unattainable. However, remember that your belief that a goal is unrealistic may be incorrect. If this were the case, you can change this belief by using imagery effectively.

Quick Summary

Goals are like a magnet; they attract your attention to keep you alive, every day in life. To achieve the goal, you need a reliable system to run your life smoothly, and to focus in order to bring you back when you get off track. To get better outcomes in life, goals, systems, and focus are like three-dimensional viewpoints, and we need all three points of view in order to balance and get real experience and optimum results.

EXPLORING ACTIVITY 4.1:
Goals, Systems, and Focus
(30 Goals, 3 Priorities, 30-Minutes Rules):

Goals, Systems, and Focus (30G-3P-30M rules)

1. Write down your 30 goals for your life, relating to your life-scale, career scale, and dream-scale, which you think are important for you to shape up your future.

2. Write down a short list of your 3 priority goals, which you should do within the next 3 months, 6months, and 12 months.

3. Identified lists, minimum continue working and deliberate practice for 30 min each day. Once you complete first 3 goal then move to next goals.

Note: Any goals more than 3 years, mark it as 3 and if 5 years mark as a 5. Follow the same method to prioritize with 3 goal and once you achieve then move to next goals. Make sure your long term goals aligned with your dream goals.

4.1 Importance of Achieving Your Goal

When you have achieved your goal, you have to take the time to enjoy the satisfaction of having done so.

Research shows that when you achieve your goal, you are 3 times happier and satisfied than others, so absorb the implications of the goal achievement, and observe the progress you have made toward other goals. If the goal was a significant one, you should reward yourself appropriately. Think of it like this: Why would you choose to ignore any accomplishments that you have made? In doing that, you are downplaying your accomplishments, which will convince you that it wasn't that important in the first place.

Limiting self-belief: My goal is too hard and takes too much time to achieve it.

Reality: You cannot do well in your life if you don't have long-term goals to achieve, which always require extra effort and practice to get results. (Deliberate Practice)

With the experience of having achieved each goal, you should next review the rest of your goal plans and see them in the following manner:

- If you achieved the goal too easily, make your next goal harder.

- If the goal took a disheartening length of time to achieve, make the next goal a little easier.

- If you learned something that would lead you to change other goals, do so.

- If while achieving the goal, you noticed a certain lacking in your skills, decide which goals to set in order to fix this.

You should keep in mind that failure to meet goals does not matter as long as you learn from it. Feed lessons learned back into your goal-setting program.

You must also remember that your goals will change as you mature. Adjust them regularly to reflect this growth in your personality. If goals no longer hold any attraction for you, let them go. Goal setting is your servant, not your master. It should bring you real pleasure, satisfaction, and a sense of achievement.

If it stops, there is no longer a point. Let's look at an example.

The best example of goal setting that you can have is to try setting your own goals. Set aside two hours to think through your lifetime goals in each of the categories. Then work back through the 10-year plan, 5-year plan, 1-year plan, 6-month plan, and even a 1-month plan.

Finally, draw up a to-do list of jobs to do tomorrow, to move toward your goals. When you do, you will soon realize that you will be on your way to using your goal-setting on a routine basis.

Key Points in Goal Setting

"The most important thing in communication is to hear what isn't said."

—Peter Drucker

Goal setting is an important method of accomplishing any lifetime achievement. However, there are some key points that you should consider before setting your goals. Let's take a look at what those are.

- Deciding what is important for you to achieve in your life, and making your choices based on this knowledge

- Separating what is important from what is irrelevant, so that your focus is in the right place

- Motivating yourself to achievement to ensure their accomplishment

- Building your self-confidence based on the measured achievement of goals

- Ensuring that your goals are your own and no one else's

You should allow yourself to enjoy the achievement of goals, and reward yourself appropriately. You must draw lessons where they are appropriate, and feed these back into future performances. In learning from mistakes and errors, you are guaranteeing future success. You would think that there would be more than five key points to goal setting, but truly, there are only five. Everything else is just a branch of the main five points. Let me show you what I mean.

4.1 YOUR GOALS:

Key point in goal setting

What this diagram shows you are the key points in setting your goals. It shows that they are the key points in the setting of your goals.

If you continue to add more branches to those four, you will see that they are all manifestations of what you are already seeing. As you continue to add more branches, you will find that all these things will tie into the first branches.

 "We are what we repeatedly do. Excellence, therefore, is not an act but a habit."

—**Aristotle**

WHY GOAL SETTING GOES WRONG

Goal setting can go wrong for a number of reasons. When these things happen, it can be a bit devastating to the self-esteem, and can make the idea of setting any new goals get muted. Before we can look into what we can do about solving these goal-setting problems, let's see what the problems would be. This section is really no more than a more detailed explanation of the above section, but I felt that it needed a section of its own to help you set your sights solely on how setting your goals can go wrong.

 Limiting self-belief: Goal setting is a boring activity, and it does not work for me.

Reality: Setting up your goals provides you clarity and direction on the way forward to your desired dream. (Reflection and Feedback)

If it seems repetitious, it is—because it is! But it is very necessary for this guide, especially for quick referencing later.

- Outcome goals can be set instead of performance goals, because it forces you to focus on the end result immediately, instead of taking your time to go through the steps of goal setting. When you set goals properly, you will be doing it in a step-by-step manner. Where you are using outcome goals, and you fail to achieve the goal for reasons outside your control, this can be very dispiriting, and can lead to loss of enthusiasm and feelings of failure. Always set performance goals instead, as this will give you a higher chance of succeeding.

- Goals can be set unrealistically high. When a goal is perceived to be unreachable, no effort will be made to achieve it. Set realistic goals so that you can best decide how to go about achieving them.

- In retrospect to the above, goals can be set so low that you feel no challenge or benefit in achieving the goal. Setting goals has been a waste of time. Always set goals that are challenging enough to be worth the effort but not out of reach.

- Goals can be so vague that they are useless. It is difficult to know whether vague goals have been achieved. If achievement can't be measured against your expectations, then your self-confidence will not benefit from goal setting, nor can you observe progress toward a greater goal. Set precise and quantitative goals.

- Goal setting can be unsystematic, sporadic, and disorganized. In this case, certain goals will be forgotten, and the achievement of goals will not be measured, and feedback will not occur in new goals. The major benefits of goal setting have been lost. Be organized and regular in the way that you use goal setting.

- Too many goals that aren't given priority may be set, leading to a feeling of overload. Remember that you deserve time to relax and enjoy being alive, and not be solely focused on your goals and achievements.

When goal setting does go wrong, not only are the benefits of goal setting lost, but the whole process of goal setting can fall into disrepute.

By avoiding these problems, and setting goals effectively as described in the previous section, you can achieve and maintain a strong forward leap into your future.

SETTING GOALS BY "QUANTUM LEAP" Approach

> *"To be successful, you must accept all challenges that come your way. You can't just accept the ones you like."*
>
> **—Mike Gafka**

One approach to goal setting for yourself and other people is the Quantum Leap approach. This tries to force intense activity by setting a goal that will need a *quantum leap* in activity to achieve it. This is a dangerous technique that should be used with a great deal of care. It is very easy for the whole process of goal setting to fall into problems when quantum leap goals are not met.

Similarly, if you are really not convinced that a goal is attainable, you will not put effort into achieving it. Doesn't all of this sound repetitious!

Business managers, using this approach, should take care that they are not shot down by someone that is firmly requesting information on how a quantum leap goal should be achieved, because then everybody suffers.

4.2 Kinds of Goals

> *"Listening is active. At its most basic level, it's about focus, paying attention."*
>
> **—Simon Sinek**

Although the concept of setting goals is easy, in general it is a great way to lead and learn your life (which was explained in the above sections). It helps to be able to set goals in specific areas of your life, separately. For example, if you want to better your career options, you will be setting goals that specifically cater to your career. Of course, career goals aren't the only goals that most people are looking to set. In this book, we will define this in more detail, but at the same time, we will brief other areas of goals, which include:

4.2 YOURGOALS LINK

Goal looks like as a block chain

Let's take a look at all of the most common goals that
you should consider, and how best to go about each one.
What would be the point in learning how to set goals in
general, and not give specific examples and instructions on
the most common goals that are set? Let's get started.

First of all, what do you think stops most people from
achieving what they want out of life? Perhaps it is a lack
of talent, lack of ability, personal circumstances, and
upbringing. I'll tell you this much: It's none of those.

The single biggest reason for an inability to reach goals
is a lack of purpose and action, or not setting them in the
first place or doing anything about it.

If you don't start in the first place, then how do you expect
to move forward? Many a lifelong adventure started with
the smallest of steps. Action is the first step to achieving
your goals. Most people are fine at choosing a goal to set,
but are inept at reaching them. You can achieve everything
you want by taking one step.

Limiting self-belief: I am doing very well
in my life and may not need to work hard.
Reality: You cannot do well in your life
if you are no longer able to manage every aspect of
your life.

One step is all you need to take—one step today, one step
next week or tomorrow—whichever is more convenient to
you. The important thing is to keep making steps once you
have started. The trouble is, often the first step is the hardest,

and the next step is just as hard. It is only after you have made a series of steps that it gets easier. You need to know the truth about what is really holding you back. Motivation and goal setting go hand in hand. The goal is your journey, and the motivation is your fuel to get there. You may have many goals but no fuel to get there. You may have gallons and gallons of fuel but no journey to go on.

What can prevent you from going on that journey? There are many more things holding you back than you realize.

You are probably the biggest cause. The way you approach a goal will ultimately affect whether you will achieve it or not. The good news is that you can break free from whatever is holding you back as goal are linked to each other.

Friends and family are next in line. They may have your best interests at heart, but their inaction is often what lies behind their advice to you. It is really common for those around you to hold you back, simply because they are not doing anything themselves. For example, if you are losing weight, some of your support system will inadvertently sabotage you by offering you food or alcohol. I'm not saying that all advice is bad; it's just that sometimes the most well-meaning of comments can empty your fuel can faster than... well, a very fast thing. You need to spot these things when someone or something is draining your fuel, and put a stop to it, either mentally or physically. You need to break free from whatever is holding you back. Now that you know this, let's get started.

4.3 Career & Professional Goals

"Work saves a man from three great evils: boredom, vice, and need."

—**Voltaire**

In architecting your future, one of the toughest issues in making a good career choice and career goal setting is identifying what it is that you want. You need to ask yourself what you want to become in the journey of your career. Even when it seems that you know what you want, you may still have doubts whether your career choice is the right one for you or not. Reaching clarity on those issues may be the most important thing you can do in your career architecting, planning, designing, and goal setting. Here are a few career goal-setting guidelines that can help to craft your journey.

Limiting self-belief: I need an engineering degree, with coding and programming skills, to have success in the digital economy.

Reality: If you have a higher degree, it is good to have but not necessary. The digital economy is opening a new dimension for growth if you have functional skills and vertical development. (*Digipreneur* are real in the digital economy.)

Most people, even very successful ones, have some periods in their career path when they seem unsure about their career choice and goals. It is totally human to feel that way. Often, such periods just come and go. For example, they come when you face some overwhelming obstacles on your way. It is all over as soon as you get through these obstacles. That situation, by itself, is not a problem of choosing a career; it is only a test of your perseverance in seeing it through—but what if those doubts persist, or if they always live somewhere in the background of your thoughts? And what if it just does not feel right? If this is the case, then it is time to look more carefully at your career choice and overall career objectives. Often, we choose or are placed in a career because it just seems like the right step to take, or that is what your studies have focused on. The only problem is that sometimes that passion, which we once had as a young adult, is now gone, or the realism of the job has taken the interest and joy out of it. That is when it is time to set a new career goal or objective. Choosing the right career goal to sink into requires a great deal of soul searching.

 "Go for it now. The future is promised to no one."

—Wayne Dyer

You need to ask yourself questions about your career and professional development, and about your drive to

move forward, and to have better purpose, performance, and results.

4.3 CAREER PROFESSIONAL DRIVERS:

These are all vital questions that you have to ask yourself before deciding. What are your career goals going to be? If you are honest with yourself, you will know exactly what direction you should be going in. Without being honest with yourself, you can't expect to better your life; you can only expect to have to ask yourself these questions all over again, until you find happiness and success in life.

CAREER GOAL SETTING PLAN & PREPARATION

The planning and preparation is a key factor to your career goal success. The following table provides you with a simple outline of the factors you may want to consider and identify when setting and analyzing your career goals in a step-by- step format.

> *"The secret to change is to focus all of your energy, not on fighting the old, but on building the new."*
>
> —**Socrates**

4.4 CAREER GOAL SETTING PLAN AND PREPARATION STEPS:

Define	Motivate	Action	Timeline	Assistance and Support	Results
Career Goal You must Define and write them down in order of priority	Benefits and Advantages of achieving this goal Listing these may help to motivate you	Key Steps That you Need to Take	When Will I do This? Give Yourself deadlines	Support and Resources (What support and from whom do I need, what resources, such as time, money, contacts)	and Reflection (Record whether you achieved the goal and what worked or did not work along the way for future reference)

The table below sort of shows you who, what, where, when, and how of your career goal setting. It is just like asking and finding the facts for a story. Journalists have to answer all of these questions in order to get the full story. That is the same thing you have to do when setting career goals. Let me show you in exact detail, in the next table.

TABLE 4.1   WHO, WHAT, WHERE, WHEN, AND HOW SUMMARY TABLE:

WHO	WHAT	WHERE	WHEN	HOW
Who will I ask for help?	What do I want the outcome to be?	Where should I start?	When should I begin?	How should I begin?
Who will benefit from my career goal?	What will I do to get started?	Where will my career goal put me in 10 years?	When do I want these goals to be reached?	How will these goals affect my future?
Who will I work with to accomplish my goal?	What will really make me happy?	Where will I apply my resources?	When will I apply my knowledge to begin attaining my goals?	How do I really feel about the goals that I have chosen?

Do you see what I'm talking about now? All of these questions have to be directed before you can begin to work on your career goals. They will take some real thought and honesty to set them properly. When you have answered these questions, you next have to begin to prioritize them. Let me show you an example.

Ryan wants to be the president of his company one day. Right now he is a mere data analyst. His company is a large technology corporation that works with computer services and security consulting. Ryan knows everything there is to know about computer services and security, and can brief and present to almost any clients and partners he works with as part of the company. He is smart, and he is efficient at using and finding hacking, securing computers, and presenting to the company's higher management and board members. His boss currently knows that Ryan is a very competent person, but he is ignoring his advice, so Ryan is not so sure how to go about getting his dream of being president of the company.

He feels that he is stuck, and he doesn't know what he should do to get out of this situation.

This is a time when Ryan should begin to assess and understand, and prioritize and decide how he can get to his goal. His ultimate goal is to be company president, and he wants to accomplish this in the next 10 years.

Ryan is currently 26 years old. Since he knows that what

and the when, he must decide everything else. I opted to
show you his possible steps, in an easy-to-read table.

TABLE 4.2   RYAN'S KEY STEPS – ACTION PLAN

	Steps for How	Steps for What	Steps for Why	Steps for When	Steps for Where
1	I will make a to-do list.	I will put my ideas for improvement in it.	I want to move up to the next position at work.	I will do this today.	I will do this in private as well as with public Collaboration.
2	How can I get noticed?	I will make a presentation showing my idea for improvement.	I can't move up if no one knows I'm there.	I will do this the day it is finished.	I will do this at work.

	Steps for How	Steps for What	Steps for Why	Steps for When	Steps for Where
3	How can I let my work be seen?	I will now show my superior my presentation.	I know my work is good and strong.	I will do this when I know my boss can't ignore me.	I will do this in my boss's office or invite him to my house.
4	How can I get the higher ups to see my work?	I will schedule time with a major company player to give my ideas.	I can't move up until I make friends with higher ups.	I will invite colleagues and higher ups to a cocktail party this weekend.	I will do this during a meeting.

	Steps for How	Steps for What	Steps for Why	Steps for When	Steps for Where
5	How can I keep moving up?	Now that I'm getting closer to higher ups, I will share my ideas verbally and get an impression.		I will do this after 3 months of making friends with higher ups.	I will bring these up at meetings with backup presentation ready if requested.

This is just a sample of the first 3 months of Ryan executing his goal to get a higher position in his company. Naturally, becoming president will take a lot longer than 3 months, but getting closer to superiors and colleagues at work, and building their trust, is a great start, as long as you don't step on anyone's toes. Over time, you can introduce your ideas and present them in a professional manner at the right time.

When you see that your company needs help on something, work in secret and bring in a finished product at the right time, or schedule private meetings with your boss.

This shows that you are not only ambitious but are also motivated and determined. It is a great way to move up in the company. In order to do this properly, you must take the steps in succession, and not try to become president in 1 year. That is unrealistic.

Although Ryan want to begin working on his long-term goal of being company president, he should also begin by setting short-term goals that will lead him there. The first goal can start with moving up one position at work, and continuing on in this method. That way, he can celebrate each promotion and advancement separately, rather than focusing only on his inability to make president right away.

From here, Ryan should just follow the step-by-step methods, mentioned in the above sections, for exact steps to attaining and setting goals. Just remember that you have to develop an action plan if you are going to succeed.

Four strategies can help you to develop an effective action plan.

   A. State your goal in very specific terms that you can accept.

   B. Plan backwards from your goal, for the best results.

   C. Confront your fears and expectations immediately and progressively.

   D. Put your plan on paper and into action as soon as possible.

Your goal:

Planning a career move is much like mapping your route for a road trip. If you don't know where you are going, you can't decide how to get there, but if you do know where you are going, you'll get there faster.

Goals like "Go back to school" are too general and not specific enough. You have to translate these goals into specific statements such as, "Enter a college accounting program by next fall," or "For the next two months, search for work in the computer securities field." You have to know exactly what you want to do and when to go about it.

Reverse Engineering – Plan Backwards:

One of the best ways to move forward is to plan backwards. Start by asking yourself if you can accomplish your goal today. If you can't, why do you think that is? What do you have to do first? Is there something you have to do before that?

Keep thinking backwards like this until you arrive at tasks you could do today. This will help you to attain the goal's starting point.

For example, if your goal is to take a two-year business administration program:

Could you start today? No,

You have to be enrolled in the program first.

Could you be enrolled today? No,

You have to apply first.

Could you apply today? No,

You have to decide which post-secondary institutions to apply to.

Could you decide today? No,

You have to do some research first and so on.

I could do this all day, but you get the point.

Don't worry if your list of things to do becomes several lists.

Deal with your fears and expectations of yourself:
Look over your list of things you will have to do to achieve your goal. Do you believe that you can do it? If you have doubts, take some time to think them through first.

Are your expectations realistic? Have you succeeded or failed at tasks that were similar to this before? What can you do to improve your chances of success this time around?

For example, if there is a good chance you will not follow through with your plans, you have to ask yourself why.

Are you a professional procrastinator? If so, what can you do to make sure that you will keep going until you reach your goal? Are you afraid of failing? If so, work at improving the skills you will need. Or test the waters by taking an evening or distance education course before you sign up for a whole program. If you are having trouble identifying your fears or figuring out how to deal with them, talk to people you trust. Ask for their suggestions, but always make your own decisions.

Put your plan into action from a to-do list:
By this stage, you probably have more than one list of things to do and, if it is necessary, some plans for avoiding or dealing with potential problems. Now you need to put them all together into one comprehensive plan. You must list tasks in the order in which you must complete them, and set deadlines for the completion of any major plans.

Successful career planners keep themselves on track using a variety of methods, such as:

- Marking tasks on a monthly calendar (noting important dates such as application deadlines or action plans)
- Making weekly or daily lists of things to do, and crossing off tasks as they are completed
- Using a computer program to create timeline charts, which give you your time limits for task completion
- Using a commercial appointment book or a notebook, or even a palm pilot, with a new page for each day or week

Use whatever methods work best for you. If it is absolutely necessary, ask a friend to check on your progress occasionally, or to question you on your successes, because you are more likely to get things done if you know that you'll be asked about it.

Now you have learned all that you could want in order to set successful career goals. If you follow the things in this section, and have remembered the previous sections, you will do just fine, because there is nothing to hold you back now.

Quick Summary

In your career, goal setting is the biggest milestone in your life, where you spend most of your time thinking about your vision, planning, and taking action to achieve meaningful life goals. You analyze your career and professional drivers, and follow through to achieve success. Goal setting in your career, for the short term and the long term, are both key success factors. During the planning and preparation phase of your career, the 5 phases are: a) Define; b) Motivate; c) Action; d) Timeline; e) Assistance and support; and f) Results. Ryan has a great challenge to drive his career growth quickly and fast forward in his early career, and we have discussed a step-by-step plan and his strategy leading toward success in his career. The four important key steps are: 1) State your goal very specifically; the more specific you are, the more clarity you have of your goal. 2) Plan backward, discussed as reverse engineering. 3) Confront your fears; fear is the biggest disease of attitude in career planning. 4) Always put your plan on paper to have clarity with vision actions.

4.4 Health & Fitness Goals

To be healthy, we need to flow in rhythm with our natural cycle, and exercise. If we are in tune with our own wheel of success performance of health, we can encounter harsh terrain—the unforeseen bumps and dips in the road—and still remain balanced. As long as we steadily encourage our body's natural equilibrium through how we live, what we eat, and how we move and think, we will maintain a good level of health, with very little conscious effort.

"You can't have a positive life and a negative mind."

—**Joyce Meyer**

Before beginning any fitness program, you need to decide what it is you want out of it. Do you want to improve your appearance or your physical skills, or to build endurance, flexibility, and strength? Are you trying to lose weight? Make sure that the activities you pick meet the goals for what you want to get out of it.

Set Yourself up for Success

>
> **Limiting self-belief:** I am very young and may not need to work out extensively.
>
> **Reality:** Your habits to be healthy start at an early age and continue for life. That is the reason we say, "Healthy mind, healthy body."

Growth mindsets

It's important not to undermine yourself with goals that are too long-term or impossible to attain.

For example, "I want to lose all my extra weight before summer" is too unrealistic; particularly if you have a great deal of weight to lose, and summer is 3 months away. There are seven to eight basic factors for your health performance speedo meter, which includes analyzing, monitoring, and measuring to keep up your health, and to be able to expect optimum performance for life. I have written a brief description, and if you need a better life, you need to measure the following:

Body Fat: The body fat percentage (BFP) of humans is the total mass of fat divided by total body mass, multiplied by 100. Body fat is made up of essential body fat and stored body fat. Essential body fat is necessary to maintain life and reproductive functions. The percentages of essential body fat for women is greater than that for men, due to the demands of childbearing and other hormonal functions. Stored body fat consists of fat accumulation in the adipose tissue, part of which protects the internal organs in the chest and abdomen. A number of methods are available for determining body fat percentage, such as measurement with calipers, or through the use of bioelectrical impedance analysis. The body fat percentage is a measure of fitness level, since it is the only body measurement that directly calculates a person's relative body composition, without regard to height and weight.

Body Weight: Body weight refers to a person's mass or weight, and it is measured in kilograms or pounds, which is a measure of mass throughout the world. Excess or reduced body weight is regarded as an indicator of determining a person's health, with body volume measurement providing an extra dimension by calculating the distribution of body weight. One of the most common questions we ask is: "How much should I weigh?" To determine how much you should weigh (your ideal body weight), several factors should be considered, including age, muscle-fat ratio, height, sex, and bone density.

Your BMI: Body mass index (BMI) is a person's weight in kilograms, divided by the square of the person's height in meters. A high BMI can be an indicator of high body fatness. BMI can be used to screen for weight categories that may lead to health problems, but it is not diagnostic of the body fatness or health of an individual. Body weight and BMI are interlinked to each other, and some health professionals suggest that calculating your body mass index is the best way to decide whether your body weight is ideal. Other views are that BMI is inaccurate, as it does not account for muscle mass, and that the waist-hip ratio is a better method.

Water: In physiology, body water is the water content that is contained in the tissues, the blood, and elsewhere. The percentages of body water contained in various fluid compartments add up to the total body water (TBW). This water makes up a significant fraction of the human body, both by weight and by volume. Ensuring the right amount of body water is part of fluid balance, an aspects of homeostasis.

SPO2 (Oxygen saturation in your body): SPO2 is also called pulse oximetry, which is a noninvasive method for monitoring a person's oxygen saturation (SO2). Though it's reading of (SO2) peripheral oxygen saturation is not always identical to the more desirable reading of (SaO2) arterial oxygen saturation from arterial blood gas analysis, the two are correlated well enough that the safe, convenient, noninvasive, inexpensive pulse oximetry method is valuable for measuring oxygen saturation in clinical use.

Muscle Mass/Physique Rating: The muscle mass, or physique rating, is the assessment of muscle and body fat levels. It rates the result as one of the types. The physique rating gives an indication of what type of body you have. When you start exercising and eating healthier, it can often take a while before you see the actual result. With the physique rating, you can get insights in your fat levels and your muscle mass. This also works the other way around. For example, your physical appearance might look good, while your (visceral) fat level has increased. The physique rating metric on your body composition monitoring gives an indication of your actual performance, and you can fine-tune as required.

Metabolic Age/Basal Metabolic Rate: Metabolism comprises the processes that the body needs to function. The basal metabolic rate is the amount of energy per unit time that a person needs to keep the body functioning at rest. Some of those processes are breathing, blood circulation, controlling body temperature, cell growth, brain and nerve function, and the contraction of muscles. The basal metabolic rate (MBR) affects the rate that a person burns calories and, ultimately, whether that individual maintains, gains, or loses weight. The basal metabolic rate accounts for about 60 to 75% of the daily calorie expenditure by individuals. It is influenced by several factors. BMR typically declines by 1 to 2% per decade after age 20, mostly due to loss of fat-free mass, although the variability between individuals is high.

The basal metabolic rate (BMR) is the rate of energy expenditure per unit time by endothermic animals at rest. It is reported in energy units per unit, ranging from watt (joule/second) to ml O2/min or joule per hour per kg body mass J/(h kg).

Bone Mass: Bone mineral density (BMD) is the amount of bone mineral in bone tissue. The concept is of mass of mineral per volume of bone (related to density in the physics sense), although clinically it is measured by proxy according to optical density per square centimeter of bone surface upon imaging. Bone density measurement is used in clinical medicine as an indirect indicator of osteoporosis and fracture risk, and measurement is non-invasive. The measurements are most commonly made over the lumbar spine and over the upper part of hip.

Visceral Fats: Visceral fat is a type of body fat that is stored within the abdominal cavity. It's located near several vital organs, including the liver, stomach, and intestines. It can also build up in the arteries. Visceral fat is sometime referred to as "active fat," because it can actively increase the risk of serious health problems. If you have some belly fat, that's not necessarily visceral fat. Belly fat can also be subcutaneous fat, stored just under the skin. Subcutaneous fat, the type of fat also found in the arms and legs, is easier to see. Visceral fat is actually inside the abdominal cavity, and it isn't easily seen. The only way to definitively diagnose visceral fat is with a CT or MRI scan. However, these are expensive and time-consuming procedures.

Instead, medical providers will typically use general guidelines to evaluate your visceral fat and the health risks it poses to your body. Harvard Health, for example, says that about 10 percent of all body fat is visceral fat. If you calculate your total body fat and then take 10 percent of it, you can estimate your amount of visceral fat.

An easy way to tell if you may be at risk is by measuring your waist size. According to Harvard Women's Health Watch and the Harvard T.H. Chan School of Public Health, if you are a woman and your waist measures 35 inches or larger, you are at risk for health problems from visceral fat. The same Harvard T.H. Chan School of Public Health article notes that men are at risk for health problems when their waist measures 40 inches or larger.

All the information provided above is not to make you a health expert but to make you aware of your physicality and physiology, so that you can keep up with your health goals that are necessary to take care of yourself, your family, and career progression, and to keep up with your daily life.

This is for you, and you will not get a prize, but it will

help you to be self-satisfied; so please review your health performance speedo meter, and remember: the larger the wheel, the better and healthier you are—and if you are not, then take an action, commit to it, and improve on it.

4.5 HEALTH PERFORMANCE SPEEDO METER

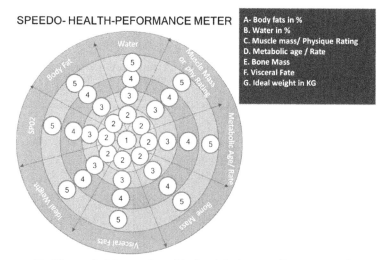

Health speedo Meter to have Ideal weight in according to age and you caliber as you desire.

Too often, goals are an end result of whatever program we choose, and not a part of it. You have to make goals an active part of your life by creating goals that lead to the next goal that works best. It is just like the backwards technique mentioned in the above section. For instance, setting a goal to lose 10 pounds puts the goal at the end, without putting too much pressure on you right away. You can add to this goal once it is achieved, and so on.

Setting a goal to join an aerobics class, and to attend it

three times a week, makes the weight loss goal a part of the program. You will have set a goal that is achievable almost immediately. This gives you a sense of accomplishment, which is an incentive to setting and achieving the next goal.

Limiting self-belief: I am doing very well in my life and may need to work hard.

Reality: You cannot do well in your life if you are no longer able to manage every aspect of your life.

Keep your achievement record:

Write your goals down so that you have something to look forward to, as well as to look back on. To begin, map out no more than eight weeks of activities toward your first fitness goal.

Working within your lifestyle, decide on a regular program. It's not necessary to work out every day, especially when beginning a new program, as your body is not used to the stress. Our bodies become tired if expected to do hard work seven days a week. Exercising every other day is a safe and realistic goal. Keep track of how much time you want to spend doing an activity, followed by how much time you will actually spend on it.

Not everyone is looking at fitness and health to lose weight. Perhaps you are just looking to better your health.

In this case, you should think of this: We tend to focus most on the area of our health in our lives, when our health is already failing or less than stellar. Unfortunately, it may sometimes take a life threatening event, illness, or some type of physical rehabilitation to give us a wakeup call to make tough changes in our current health habits. We try to follow through on sound health principles such as enough sleep, a healthy diet, and plenty of exercise, yet we may not have the time in our busy schedule, or have strong enough will power to implement a balanced and healthy lifestyle. With the pressures of the fast-paced world in which we live, stress can set in and can take its toll. These days, we are on the road more often. What that means is that we are eating on the road as well, which doesn't always offer us the best or healthiest choices.

We are lucky to get six or maybe seven hours of sleep per night, while we now work at least six days per week.

The old saying, "At least I have my health," is finally starting to mean something to a great deal of people. You might be wondering what you can do to improve your health.

The first thing to do is to prioritize what is most important to you in your own individual lifestyle.

You can begin by asking yourself these questions:

1. What is my current exercise goal this month, or do I even have one?
2. What gets in my way when starting or continuing a balanced health maintenance program?
3. What is my target weight and my plan and timeframe to get there?
4. How can I improve on getting more sleep?

5. What are my ideal overall appearance hopes?

6. Would a personal trainer help me develop and reach my goals more effectively, and can I afford one?

7. What meals should I eat each month? How can I eat healthier, and what can I change in order to eat healthier without getting bored?

8. What books and classes can I take to improve upon my health?

9. Is it time for me to go in for a complete physical? When was the last one that I had?

10. How can I reduce or completely eliminate alcohol, chemical dependencies, and/or smoking?

11. What ways may I be able to cook in a healthier manner?

12. How can I improve my current heart rate, blood pressure, and cholesterol counts?

The fact of the matter is that it doesn't matter what your fitness/health goals are. If you have read the above sections on setting goals properly, and this section about fitness and health, you are ready to go. You have to be honest with yourself at all times when it comes to your personal goals. Are you unsure as to what constitutes good and balanced nutrition? You should also consult a doctor before making any changes to your diet or exercise regimen, to ensure that you will not harm yourself, and focus on regular exercise.

Exercise:

What is exercise? The World Health Organization (WHO, 2011) says, "Physical activity is defined as any bodily movement produced by skeletal muscles that requires energy expenditure."

Exercise helps to improve the immune system. With regular exercise, it makes us less likely to suffer from colds and flu, as well as degenerative disorders such as cancer. It lowers cholesterol and, most importantly, it will help to reduce the overall cholesterol level. Exercise improves the ratio of good to bad fats, and improves existing conditions such as arthritis, cancer, osteoporosis, and many others.

Research was done by neuroscientist, Wendy Suzuki, to discuss the science of how working out and doing exercise boosts your mood and memory, and protects your brain against neurodegenerative diseases like Alzheimer's.

(Refer to YouTube: The Brain-Changing Benefits of Exercise, by Wendy Suzuki.)

Exercise helps prevent conditions such as diabetes, depression, and Alzheimer's. Seven hours of brisk walking every week has been shown to lower the rate of colorectal cancer by 40% (Halle and Schenberg 2009). "Up to a third of breast cancer cases could be avoided if women in Western countries exercised more." (La Vecchia)

IMPROVE YOUR MOOD: Because of the effect it has on your endpoints, exercise can help your mood and combat depression and anxiety.

PREVENT STROKE: Research has shown that exercise can reduce the risk of suffering and dying from a stroke, by 27%, and can cut the risk of cerebral hemorrhage in men by 40% (Reimers, Knapp, and Reimers 2009). Exercise also releases frustration, tension, and anger. There are various kinds of exercise— heavyweight, lightweight, and cardio—but the most common forms of exercise are swimming, cycling, Yoga, dancing, Tai Chi, and Qi Gong, and it requires regular practice to be healthy.

Quick Summary
In this chapter, we have discussed the importance of health and setting goals that suit your daily performance. Health goals also help you to be optimistic by setting up realistic goals to achieve your weight, by yoga, regular exercise, and active social activities. We also discussed assessing your current health situation by using the Health Speedo Meter, and deciding your desired health goals to take a proactive action to achieve and maintain them. As the saying goes, "Health is wealth." Your lifestyle depends on your health. If you have good health, you can achieve many things in your life.

EXPLORING ACTIVITY 4.2:
Health and Fitness

---

1. Please assess your health and wellness through the Health Speedo Success Meter.

2. Analyze your eating style vs health style vs lifestyle, and fine-tune as per your convenience and goals, and discuss with your friends, family, and doctors.

3. Please keep track of FLY SPEEDO HEALTH METER, and do periodic checks.

EXPLORING ACTIVITY 4.3:
Sample Health Logs

Name: _____

Age:_____

Current Weight: _____

Ideal Weight:_____

Height:_____

BMI: _____

Body Fat %: _____

Water %: _____

Body Oxygen Saturation (SPO2) %: _____

Muscle Mass/Physique Rating:_____

Metabolic Age /B. Metabolic Rate: _____

Bone Mass: _____

Visceral Fat: _____

Your Improvement Goals, Observation, and
Commitment:

4.5 Relationship Goals

> *"I define connection as the energy that exists between people when they feel seen, heard, and valued; when they can give and receive without judgment, and when they derive sustenance and strength from the relationship."*
>
> —**Brene Brown**

Relationship goals, for yourself and toward your external world, are both important to align your life to be successful. In order for a relationship to be satisfying, those involved in it must set clear goals for it. Your relationship with your inner circle and your external relationships, are two different things. Most people enter into a relationship with a vague idea of what they want out of it. When pressed, they often are unable to specify their goals for the relationship in the long term.

"Taking care of your body and mind is important, but tending to your relationships is a form of self-care too. That, I think, is the revelation." The study revealed that having close relationships, more so than money or fame, is what keeps people happy throughout their lives. Those ties protect people from discontentment in their lives, and help to delay mental and physical decline. It is a better predictor of a long and happy life than even your genes would be. That is one of the biggest reasons that relationships play a key role for architecting your future and defining your goals.

"Loneliness kills. It's as powerful as smoking or alcoholism."

—**Robert Waldinger**

Relationship goals can be stated or written, but they should be agreed upon by the partners at the beginning of the relationship. Relationship goals sometimes are dictated by behavior, for the short term. However, for a relationship to work, the goals stated should be only those on which both partners can agree, and which are long-term. Your relationship goals should be kept in a safe place and reviewed annually, as your needs tend to change annually. During the annual review, the goals can be modified, and the objectives to be achieved for the next year can be identified. Relationship goals should be long-term, but they should be general enough to give the partners enough latitude to be satisfying and easy to achieve. Annual objectives based on these goals can be more specific and short-term, motivating the partners to successfully achieving them within the year. Relationship goals should be developed to cover key issues involved in the relationship, but they can cover any area of human behavior. In order to best know how and what goals need to be set, you have to ask yourself a variety of questions to get to know yourself, your partner, and your priorities. I would recommend that you do a little quiz, and I am sure you will find it interesting to explore your compatibility and see how it goes:

The Relationship Goal Setting Quiz:

1. How can we best nurture our support for one another?

2. How will we communicate with one another on a daily basis?

3. How dependent will we be on one another, and is it healthy?

4. How can we give our mutual intimacy a boost in the relationship?

5. How long do we intend our relationship to last; for example, do we want to get married?

6. How will we ensure that we respect each other's rights in this relationship?

7. How will we help one another "grow" in this relationship?

8. How can we keep the fun in our relationship?

9. How will we include others in our relationship without losing our support for one another?

10. How should or will we approach problems in our relationship?

11. How will we solve problems?

12. How are we going to handle various differences of opinion?

13. How will we handle irritation with one another, and is it worth the effort?

14. How are we going to handle fights and bring them to a healthy resolution?

15. At what point will we seek help for ourselves if our fighting gets out of hand, or will we even bother? For example, will we seek counseling together?

16. Will we agree to disagree?

17. How can we ensure mutual growth in this relationship?

18. How open are we to taking joint and individual responsibility for our relationship?

19. How can we ensure that our individuality doesn't get lost in this relationship?

20. How open are we to being assertive in our relationship?

21. How can we use our unique, individual personalities to help each other and our relationship to grow?

22. What steps will we take if one or both of us begins to feel smothered by the relationship?

23. What steps are we willing to take if one or both of us has the need for mental health assistance?

24. How are we going to promote each other's physical health, and will we be supportive of each other?

25. What steps can we take to handle jealousy, a sense of competition, or resentment toward one another?

26. How are we going to make time to do all the things we want to do?

27. How are we going to arrange our schedules so that we can pursue our unique, individual interests and still spend quality time together?

28. How free are we to pursue our distinct interests and friends?

29. How committed are we to setting up long-range relationship goals and short-range objectives to reach those goals?

30. How committed are we to setting up times in which we can nourish one another and keep our relationship on track?

31. How can we structure ways to get the "required" relationship maintenance tasks?

32. How can we delegate the maintenance tasks so that neither of us feels that we are doing too much?

33. What place will religion, hobbies, sports, and outside interests have in our relationship?

34. How important are those things to our relationship?

35. Can we nurture our differences?

I know that this sounds funny, and it may seem like a lot of questions to answer, but it's fun. And seriously, if we are all realistic, all of these questions matter in the short and long term. If you are not brutally honest enough to take this little quiz seriously, how can you expect to take a long-term relationship seriously, and be committed?

STEPS TO CALCULATE YOUR RELATIONSHIP SCORE:

How to calculate your compatible and comparable score:

For every same answer, give yourself 1 point (+1 point).

For every different answer, take 1 point away (–1 point).

If you and your partner score below 17,

It doesn't mean that you should break up; it just means that you both have to sit down and decide on your personal relationship goals together, and form a compromise that you can both agree on with each other.

All relationships require compromise by both parties if they are going to be successful.

You just need to re-evaluate what your goals are going to be. If you and your partner scored above 17, it simply means that you are on the right track and are likely looking to get the same things out of the relationship. You will still have to compromise a bit (you are human) to keep the relationship going, but you are heading in the right direction. What you need to realize is that setting relationship goals is best when both parties are involved in the process. If only one is working for the betterment of the relationship, it is doomed to fail anyway, because one partner will always feel overworked in the relationship. Setting relationship goals is no different than setting up any other types of goals, such as career, finance, or health goals. The biggest difference is that you generally have to set your goals with the other person involved; they are joint goals with common objectives, which will give you a better purpose for your life and architecting your future.

Setting relationship goals works for all types of relationships, be it friendships, family, colleagues, or partners.

You can try to set the goals and work on them yourself, but it will be very difficult and sometime quite unsatisfying. That is why the key to setting relationship goals is to have the full co-operation and support of those who are already in a relationship such as you would like to have. You want to get the most out of the relationship, and it should be a long-term objective.

Other than that, you can simply follow the steps in the method of achieving your goals, as was mentioned in the above section on how to set goals effectively and efficiently.

Quick Summary

In this chapter, relationship goals are focused on your life partner and selecting your partner's perspective. These are specific considerations, as today's research shows more divorces than marriages. This means there are not as many long-term commitments, and it has become so dynamic that setting relationship goals in life is one of the most challenging goals, and they are changing frequently. We have analyzed the 35 questions in the quick relationship self-quiz, in order to know which direction you are heading. The relationship quiz is interesting an important because it defines your future, based on current decisions, and requires measured and continued balance. The strategy is to set sustainable and valuable relationship goals, for life and for architecting your future, so that you can decide today and get married tomorrow.

EXPLORING ACTIVITY 4.4: Relationships

1. Please do your relationship quiz honestly, and analyze how you build and support relationships, and how you want people to treat you on your relationship with mutual respect.

2. Identify the area you want to improve, in which you need support.

3. Set your personal goal, target your relationship improvement plan, and timeline to achieve it. Remember relationship improvement required quality time, more time you spend the better your relationship will be.

4.6 Financial Goals

Finance and personal economy play a key role in everyone's success in life, for the job-scale, career-scale, and dream-scale. If you don't plan strategies and basic financial literacy, you will struggle throughout your life. No matter what your age is, or what your current situation looks like, you should always be setting your financial goals to help guide you to make wiser decisions, and most importantly, to influence your financial behavior. Whether you want to save for your education or for your kids' or family's education, or for your retirement or business startup, or for your personal health and safety, don't wait to start...

The first step in personal financial planning is learning to understand the need to control your day-to-day financial affairs, to enable you to do the things that bring you satisfaction, confidence, and enjoyment. This is achieved by planning, setting a goal, and following a budget.

 Limiting self-belief: I am doing very well in my life, and my finances will be taken care of.

Reality: Understanding personal finance is the key to success in the digital era. Financial independence gives you choices of what you would like to do to architect your future. You cannot do well in your life if you are no longer able to manage every aspect of your life.

The second step in personal financial planning, and the topic of this section, is choosing and following a course toward achieving your long-term financial goals and financial freedom. As with anything else in life, without financial goals and specific plans for meeting them, you will just drift along and leave your future to chance. A wise man once said: "Most people don't plan to fail; they just fail to plan." The end result is the same, which is the failure to reach financial freedom and independence.

The third step in personal financial planning is learning how to build a financial safety net, which is like having a retirement fund for when you are no longer generating any income.

The fourth step in personal financial planning is to understand your net worth, which is your total assets minus your liabilities. This can tell you a lot about your current financial health, and help you to plan your financial future. Find out what your net worth is now. Then get in the habit of recalculating your net worth yearly, or whenever there is a significant change to your finances.

It might be tempting to skip this step, but determining your net worth may be the most important part of organizing your finances. Your net worth is the cash you could pocket if you were to sell everything you own, and pay off all of your debts. If you take a hard look and determine this simple figure, you can then work backward to create a budget, set a financial goal, track spending, and ultimately take control of your finances.

4.6 FOUR STEPS OF FINANCIAL GOALS

FOUR SIMPLE STEPS FOR SETTING FINANCIAL GOALS

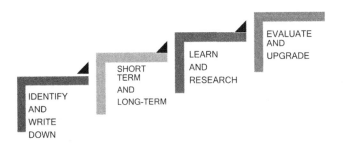

FOUR SIMPLE STEPS FOR SETTING FINANCIAL GOALS

Step 1: Identify and write down your financial goals, whether it is saving to send your kids to college or university, buying a new car, saving for a down payment on a house, going on vacation, paying off credit card debt, or planning for you and your spouse's retirement.

Step 2: Break each financial goal down into several short-term (less than 1 year), medium-term (1 to 3 years), and long-term (5 years or more) goals, which will make this process easier.

Step 3: Educate yourself and do your research. Read *Money Magazine*, or a book about investing, or surf the Internet's investment web sites. Do not be afraid of the stock market.

Yes, there is a potential for loss, but if you do your research and get a trustworthy broker, you can ensure your financial future. Just remember not to put all of your eggs in one basket.

Diversify your portfolio. With a little effort, you can learn enough to make educated decisions that will increase your net worth many times over. Then identify small, measurable steps you can take to achieve these goals, and put this action plan to work.

Step 4: Evaluate your progress as often as needed. Review your progress monthly, quarterly, or at any other interval you feel comfortable with, but at least semi-annually, to determine if your program is working. If you're not making a satisfactory amount of progress on a particular goal, re-evaluate your approach, and make changes as necessary.

There are no hard and fast rules for implementing a

financial plan. The important thing is to at least do something as opposed to nothing, and to start NOW. Sometimes when people write down their goals, they discover that some of the goals are too broad in meaning and nearly impossible to reach, while others may seem smaller in scope and easier to achieve. It is okay to dare to dream about riches, but be realistic about what you can actually do. A good idea is to break your goals down into three separate categories of time.

One more thing to remember: By placing a time frame on your goals, you are motivating yourself to get started, and helping to allow yourself the chance to succeed. Just remember that you can adjust the time frame whenever you want to.

Long-term goals (over 5 years) are those things that won't happen overnight, no matter how hard you work to achieve them. They may take a long time to accomplish (hence the reason they are called long-term goals), so give yourself a reasonable amount of time, which is based on your best estimates of what it will take to achieve them.

Examples of long-term goals might include college education for a child, a retirement plan, or purchasing a home. Whatever the case, these goals generally require longer commitments, and often more money in the end.

Intermediate-term goals (1-5 years) are the type of goals that can't be executed overnight but might not take many years to accomplish. Examples might include purchasing/replacing a car, getting an education or certification, or paying off your debts (depending on the amount), like credit cards, etc.

Short-term goals (within one year) generally take one year or less to achieve, based on the date the task is needed, the total estimated cost, and the required savings.

What are your goals? To find out, you need to make up a list, decide which timeline your goal fits into, detail the steps necessary to achieve your goals, and then take action toward reaching those goals. It's that simple.

You might be wondering where to start, when deciding how to go about your financial goals. These are some basic tips to help you in making the best choices.

After looking at these tips, it is best for you to go out and do some research to find the method(s) that suit you best.

- Begin by taking 5%–10% out of each pay check, and put it in a savings account.

- Look into different investment strategies, such as IRAs, local and global stocks, mutual funds, personal investments, etc. There are many more, and all can assist you in short and long-term goals.

- Start making a budget for yourself that leaves you with some extra money, and follow it.

- Use your coupons; that is why they are there. It seems like small savings, but added together, you could save 20–30 dollars at each trip to the market.

- Shop around for bargains.

- Do not live outside of your means.

- Work with a credit counselor to get help in lowering your monthly expenses, and get rid of your debt.

These are just some of the things that you can do when beginning to realize your financial goals. Of course, you also have to follow the steps in the above sections on how to successfully set goals. The steps to successfully set goals don't change, only the methods that you use to go about it. By that, I mean: When it is career- wise, work to get noticed; for relationships, work on maintaining your intimacy or getting it back; in financial matters, work to save and invest money, etc. It really is that easy.

Quick Summary

Financial goals are like oxygen for your life. You need to have your short-term and long-term financial goals. Financial goals that you set today may not have the same priority in the next 5 or 10 years. For example, you may have started your job, but you may want to go for higher education. As of now, you feel it is enough; but eventually, your requirements change as you progress in life. As life changes, and your personal economy changes, expect to adapt your financial goals to your new situation. So, reviewing your goals from time-to-time is key to architecting your future.

EXPLORING ACTIVITY 4.5:
Finance and Personal Economy

1. Write down all your financial goals, especially your financial planning and financial freedom goal.

   Example: If you are working and earning close to $150,000 annually, and in the case that you stop working, you need at least $100,000 a year to continue the same way in your life.

   To earn $100,000 per year as passive income, @ 5% annual interest, you need close to $2,000,000 capital worth to get a similar level of earning.

   Getting $2,000,000, in the short term, is very tough, so you need to plan long-term investment goals to achieve it. Please plan at least a dual investment strategy. One could be real estate, and another could be mutual funds or stocks, or you could establish a company based on your passion, hobby, or interest. But your goal should be to earn as early as possible, so that you are not worried about your basic needs. Then you have the choice to explore and expand your life as you like.

2. Keep your financial goal and timeline to achieve that goal, and keep track of it.

3. Get support, if required, to achieve it.

4. Appreciate whoever supports you to drive, and helps you to achieve your goals and desires in your life.

5. Please update your financial plan, and keep track of it.

4.7 Family Goals

"If you want to change the world, go home and love your family."

—**Mother Theresa**

Limiting self-belief: Let me focus on my job, career, and profession, and I will take care of my family later.

Reality: Family and career are both equally important parts of the equation when it comes to getting better results and success in the Digital economy. Research shows that distraction from social and digital media is at a peak in our history. You have less time for yourself and your family, and more time for social media and distraction.

Every family could use a little bit of help in setting family goals. Perhaps your family wants to take a really fantastic vacation together this year. three-day, romantic get-away, just for the parents, which never seems to happen; and the home improvement project that no one ever seems to have time for. Most families live on a certain budget. Living within a budget can help your family pay off those credit cards once and for all, and realize your child's dreams of going to college, or your dream of getting a bigger and better house. Perhaps your family's goal is to see your kids go from a C-average to a B, or to have more quality family time together. Maybe you want to start your own home-based business so that you can spend more time with your family. Each and every one of these worthy goals can be easily achieved in a somewhat remarkable and FUN way. In fact, when you know how, working toward a goal can be more fun than achieving the goal. If you want to add some real teamwork in your family, and deepen your familial relationships, you must set goals with your spouse and with your kids. Just make sure that anyone who participates in the goal-setting process is motivated enough to follow through. Anyone who is not fully committed to achieving the goal should not be allowed to participate or reap in the rewards. If you really want to teach your kids something worthwhile that will help with every aspect of their lives as long as they live, teach them how to set goals. Here's the goal-setting system that seems to work for everyone who's tried it. It will work with basically any goal you can imagine, and in specific, family goals that you can achieve together. It is a great way to get the whole family working together toward a positive environment. If nothing else, your family will have a great time trying.

1. Decide your dream goals.

Make a list of everything that each of you think you want... all the goals you think you want to achieve. They may involve money, material things, better relationships, a special vacation, or a change in your personal attitudes or habits.

Get some paper and a pen, and go somewhere where you can be completely alone and uninterrupted. Write down everything that comes to mind, being careful not to judge or dismiss any of your ideas. Remember that every member of the family should do this as well. You will all compare and agree to compromise on which goals to work toward first, etc.

After you have this long list of goals written down, put the list away for a few days. Some of the things you wrote may begin creating a burning energy in your mind.

Review your list in about a week, and see which of the goals you're still interested in. Anything that you don't feel strongly about should be removed from the list. Goal setting will not work if you're not really motivated to achieve the goal. Have your family members do the same. After you identify the goal, or goals that you want to work on, start writing everything down. A spiral notebook, just for your goals, might be very helpful. Write down your goal on the first page of your notebook, and you can all start formulating them in order of the least to most important.

2. Identify the obstacles that may prevent you from achieving the goal.

After you've set your goal, make a list of things that may threaten the successful achievement of the goal, and what you can do to remove those threats. For example, are you and your spouse or child fighting over some of these goals? Write down ALL the obstacles that you feel may prevent you from reaching your goal. This is a particularly magical part of goal setting because it takes all of the obstacles that seemed so huge before, and reduces them to little letters that form words on a piece of paper. Once the obstacles are clearly defined, they are, more often than not, easily solved.

3. Identify the things you need to help you achieve the goal.

After you've identified the obstacles, make a written list of the things you will need in order to achieve your goal. This list should also include the people whose cooperation can help you work toward your goal. Some of the items on this list may include some things that will represent solutions to the problems you wrote down earlier.

4. Set a date for the achievement of your goal.

Setting a date for the attainment of your goal is the ignition for the goal-seeking missile in your mind. Make sure that your date is realistic... not so soon that it's impossible, but not so delayed that it's not interesting. Make sure you write the date of your goal down next to your goal. Once you've set this date, you should never change it unless it is absolutely necessary.

5. Write down the goal. Review it often.

Once you have your goal and the date in writing, make more reminders of your goal. Put these reminders all around your house, your car, your bathroom. They will remind you of your goal and the date that the goal will be achieved by, and each time you see this information, you will be programming your mind to take action toward your goal. This is an important step.

6. Make a step-by-step plan.

First, let's review: You know what you want, and you know you want it badly.

You have identified the problems you need to remove before you can achieve your goal, and you know whose help and cooperation you will need. You know the date for the attainment of the goal. Now, make a step-by-step action plan. Write down every little thing, no matter how small, that you must do in order to reach your goal.

Break the project into the tiniest of pieces... If you have a complicated list, jot down all the ideas that come to mind, and then put them in date sequence later.

If necessary, number them and then type them into a word processor, or re-write them in date sequence. Each item should also have a deadline for accomplishment, so that you can see that you're on target along the way.

This is an important part of your goal achievement, so don't cut corners on your plan, especially if it is a complicated goal or there are a lot of obstacles to overcome.

7. Follow your Plan.

This is the fun part, because after you've set and hit your first goal, you'll know that all you have to do to achieve your goal is to follow your plan! Review your plan every single day. Work on something on your list every single day. Stay on schedule. Don't fall behind. Review your goal and the deadline. Mark items off the list as you accomplish them.

You can't control every aspect of your future, of course, but you will be surprised how many things you really can control with these effective goal-setting techniques. This is a great way to get the family working together and doing something positive that is for the benefit of all. If nothing else, it will give you all the time spent together to achieve one or more goals, and you will definitely be together.

Quick Summary

Family goals are a priority for life, and we have discussed 7 steps to achieve your goals for your family. Those steps are: a) choose your family's dream goal wisely, and make sure it is important for you and your family. b) Identify the obstacles and how you are going to manage them. c) Select kinds of goals. d) Define the timeline. Without a timeline, there is no commitment, and nothing works. e) Write it and track it. f) Prioritize based on purpose. g) Commit to yourself. Self-commitment and brutal honesty always make you responsible for architecting the future for your family.

EXPLORING ACTIVITY 4.6:
Family Goals

1. Write down all your family goals for your life, and how they relate to your life-scale, career-scale, and dream-scale.

2. Write down all your goals, with the timeline and support required to achieve your family goals.

3. Write down the support required to achieve each goal, being brutally honest and transparent. If you need any help for other family members, please don't hesitate to share and seek help.

4. Write down your lifestyle goal and how you would like to live your family life, and what legacy you would like to leave for your family.

4.8 Art and Play Goals

Life is busy. We get it. But carving out time for you're art, play, and hobbies is really important.

Why It Matters

Hobbies help us develop new skills, learn new things, and even make new friends. Plus, taking time out for your favorite hobby is a great stress reducer and confidence builder, and this could be your ultimate choice of career too.

"Don't look at your feet to see if you are doing it right. Just dance."

—**Anne Lamott**

Maya is currently working for one of the world's largest global consulting firms, based out of Singapore. She graduated from one of the top law schools in Europe, and is academically the best performer in her domain, with 15 years of expertise in the corporate world. She always felt stressed and that something was missing. It was required that she consistently travel, and upgrade her skills globally in consumer and corporate industries. The good part is that she has a huge interest and a hidden talent in arts and paining, and she does this in her free time. She always practices during her painting in free time, and she has an interest in teaching kid's arts and painting,

Limiting self-belief: Let me work hard, and then I will be happy and enjoy my life...

Reality: There is no perfect time; every moment is a perfect moment, and you need to enjoy and give 100% to be present in that moment, to get exponential growth. Mindfulness

Are you the kind of person that always admired the artistic people of the world, like singers, actors, writers, and poets, painters, and sports persons? Have you always wondered what masterpieces you could create if you only had the time? Chances are, if you are looking to set artistic goals, you already have the passion, interest, and talents. If not, perhaps part of your goal is to go to school for it. Whatever the reason or skill level you are at, you too can make an artistic achievement, if you know how to set the goal and how to apply it. Before trying to achieve your artistic goals, you should first be certain that you know all of the steps needed to begin. You should also know what your personal skill level is, so that you can begin chasing that artistic goal on the right track from the beginning.

Not sure where to start? Ask yourself: What's the one thing you've always wanted to learn? Or is there an old hobby you once enjoyed... you know, before life got busy? Think of something that makes you feel excited and happy, and link it to a talent stake platform (TSP). The TSP is where you develop your 6 senses and become ready to face the world, with new opportunities.

Ask yourself these specific questions before deep diving and sinking into it.

- What style of art and play most interests me (for example, music, painting, writing, sports, video games, puzzles, wildlife, etc.)?
- What is my current skill level (physically, mentally, and emotionally)?
- Do I want to pursue it as a hobby, or possibly as an alternative career?
- Do I need to go to school or a vocational training course?
- Am I looking for certification or just basic skills?
- Do I have the time to go to school or a training course?
- Am I just trying to relieve stress, or to create a masterpiece or salable work for people, with my expertise in art?
- How much does doing this mean to me?
- Is this really something that I want to pursue for the long term?
- Will doing this make me happy and get me mindfulness?

When deciding on setting artistic goals, you must follow the step-by-step method in the above sections. The most important thing that you can do to help you set and reach your artistic goals is to stick to it. That's right; the best thing that you can do to achieve your artistic goals is to persevere. Art consists of 90% inspiration and 10% perspiration. Just inspire yourself in the best ways that suit you. If you follow our guide, and keep your focus on your goals, you will succeed. I guarantee it. You will be feeling excited.

Example of my quick (7 days/daily (7DD) plan) tips for your artistic and playful plan:

TABLE 4.3 7-DAY/DAILY ARTISTIC AND PLAYFUL PLAN:

Monday: Prioritize it	It might go without saying, but make your hobby a priority! If you're having trouble finding time, cut something else out. Do you need to go on social media today? Can you wake up an hour earlier?
Tuesday: Enjoy it in spurts	Indulge in your hobby for short "spurts" of time. For example, cook with just 5 ingredients, not 10. Bike the shorter loop. Or walk for just 10 minutes.
Wednesday: Designate a space	Do you have a special area just for your hobby? Even if it's the corner of a spare bedroom, it gives you a space to store your materials and to focus.
Thursday: Find a friend	Saturday or Sunday morning yoga with a friend? Yes, please! Finding time for your hobby is a lot easier (and more fun) if you do it with a friend.

Friday: Ditch digital distractions	Struggling to find time for your hobby? Power off electronics! Swap the 30 to 60 minutes you spend browsing the web, for your hobby.
Saturday : Get paid for your hobby	Some hobbies, like crafting, working on cars, writing, painting, or music, can earn you money. When you get paid to do what you love, you'll always find a way to make time in your day!
Sunday: Try something new	It's easier to reserve time for a hobby when it's new and exciting! Take up photography or mountain biking. Start a book club. Keep trying until you find something you enjoy!

Quick Summary

Arts and Play has a virtual role in the digital era, to keep you re-energized and also on your best, joyful, fun-loving career-scale. In the case of Maya, despite having a high-performing, global professional career, she has decided to find an alternative career in art and play. She currently enjoying, feel happy and becoming wiser in her career.

EXPLORING ACTIVITY 4.7:
Art and Play Goal

1. Write down all your art and play goals for your life, relating to your life, career, and dream-scales.

2. Write down all your goals, with a timeline and the support required to achieve the goal.

3. Write down the support required to achieve your goal, and how to celebrate after achieving your goal.

4. Write down your lifestyle goal and how you would like to live your life.

4.9 Goal Setting do's & Don'ts: Awareness of Your Goals

Limiting self-belief: Goal setting does not work for me; I have tried many times.

Reality: To make your goal setting work, you need to know what activities you should do and what you should not do. It requires clarity and ownership to achieve your result.

For the purposes of this guide, I thought it would be a good idea to discuss and decide how a do's and don'ts category could help you get to the nitty-gritty, in a nice and quick manner. Think about it; if you are reading this, you want to start setting goals and achieving them now, not later. This can be a quick guide for re-reading later.

TABLE 4.4   DO'S and DON'TS OF
GOAL SETTING

Do's	Don'ts
❖ Visualize your desired outcome.	❖ Go into your goal with a defeatist attitude.
❖ Write down your course of action in an easy, step-by-step format that can be checked off with each accomplishment.	❖ Try to memorize all of the steps, as most will be forgotten.
❖ Think positive all the time.	❖ Let yourself be overcome with the negatives or setbacks.
❖ Surround yourself with motivating factors, and keep them in easy-to- spot locations.	❖ Forget the reason why you have set up your goals in the first place.

Do's	Don'ts
❖ Set your plan of action as soon as you know what you want, and start right away.	❖ Procrastinate on beginning your course of action.
❖ Be realistic in setting your goals.	❖ Set your goals too high to achieve them.
❖ Be specific in the goals you choose.	❖ Set goals that are too vague.
❖ Learn to be organized in your thinking patterns.	❖ Let anything stand in the way of achieving your goals.
❖ Make an effort to keep track of all of your achievements.	❖ Downplay your achievements; you are keeping yourself motivated.
❖ Share your achievements with those around you.	❖ Let yourself get off track; stay focused on your goals!

Now you can understand what the purpose is of having a goal, and what kind of goal you can set for your life. All these do's and don'ts are good for knowing what to do next with your career, goals, and future. The best way to architect your future is to have multiple options of creation for your life, which provides you direction on your job view, career view, and dream view, and provides you a way forward, looking beyond your day-to-day worries.

Four emotions to success:

1. Discuss (I have it): You decide that you are not leaving like this, by your choice.

2. Decision (inner-civil war): If it's easy, it's easy; if it's hard, it's hard. Get it done.

3. Desire (comes from inside): Desire can be triggered, by a book, seminar, or friends. Welcome every human experience, even bad experiences.

4. Result (I will): Nothing can resist human will; either I will do it or die. A man says that he will climb a mountain. He promises himself that he will never give up.

Action: You must do something to move on.

Quick Summary

Goal setting do's and don'ts are the key to understanding and analyzing, to achieve your goal for success. Sometimes it's more important not to do things, if you can't move forward in goal setting.

Life has both sweet sugar and strychnine, so we need to be careful and watchful at the same time.

Important Lessons: Stand guard at the door of your mind while setting up your goals—*watch your coffee every day*. You decide what you feed your mental faculties, as you will be left with the results for architecting your future; so make sure that you plan ahead.

DESIGN
"I am an Architect of my Future;
I Discover, Design,
and Choose to Build IT"

Architecting Lives

CHAPTER 5

Creating architecture involves "looking to the future."

An architect always has a vision to see the complete picture, based on a goal. He applies architectural thinking to plan A and B, which includes a short-term goal to solve a problem, and a long-term strategy to achieve the desired outcome. This is more art than science, and most of the time it works well in a pragmatic approach to life, as a prototype and proof of concepts. So far, we have discussed your life and the understanding of your purpose in life, as well as constructing, goal setting, and kinds of goals. Going forward, you need to apply architectural thinking as a growth mindset. The career and life that you are planning for the future requires multiple roles to be played within your career. You will also observe significant change, resilience, and growth. It's also an alignment with your dream views.

The simple object of architecting your life is to have multiple options so that you can take multiple, smaller career projects, and align them with your dream projects. In industry, it's called a solution approach, where you are creating multiple solutions for a specific problem, but you are keeping your goal in the big picture of your life, as a future goal. Life also requires a similar approach and thought process. You need to have a solution, or career solution, for your life, which can help to build your dream view, as well as an alternative career solution. In life, you always have a plan, but it always goes off in every direction when you have too much information, and too many options and plans. So do not worry; you will be able to "architect your life" at any stage, and achieve the dream view of your life.

Working with all age groups, in various countries, we have found that people initially go wrong on planning, but as an execution process start, it aligned well with long-term goals, and they get successful results with persistence. It's called an *iterative process*, and you can modify and restart again and again from any point in time. It's never too late, and that is why architecting your life is iterative. The architecture of your life is bound to change, and your continued needs have to be refined and re-tuned till you get the best for your life.

Vikas was stressed out after completing his global MBA. He worked in a prestigious company for 5 years, as a software quality analyst, and then he decided to do a full time MBA so that he would get global learning experience and exposure for the next level, and a faster career move. As he already had software experience and business skills, he could qualify to apply his technical skills to a management degree. He had a goal to be in a business organization, and his long-term dream view was to become a digital entrepreneur with his own company, and to support his mother's business and finally achieve his dream of being settled in Australia.

In his final year, he has done two internships, one in Sydney, Australia, and the other in Dubai, UAE but in his final semester, he didn't get selected for any campus recruitment for a final job, and he was feeling really stressed, as he was really only looking for a business consultant job opportunity, without looking at alternatives options.

We met to discuss some formal guidance and to provide career advice, as well as provide a direction to help him define and architect his career, for a short-term objective and a long-term goal. After my 2 to 3 hours of discussion, a few questions and answers, and understanding his longer career and dream-scales, we discussed and agreed, based on a **Talent Stack Platform (TSP)**, to have a dual competency approach to apply architecting to his future, so that he could get an immediate job, as well as create a path for long-term success.

After assessment and joint discovery, he had two job options and one dream-scale as a final goal in his career. This was a very well aligned career path to purpose, with his dream-scale and future plan.

First, He has done his global MBA, so he is looking a business consultant job to fulfill his immediate short-term goal requirements.

Second, Since he has 5 years of experience in a technical analyst role, he could have a plan B as an alternative option in case he didn't get a business consultant role overseas or in any global company. He could then fall back to a QA business consultant role at any time.

Third, In the long term, he would like to become a self-made digital entrepreneur; but before that, he

would like to get good experience and exposure in
the business area, as he already has a good education.
He would like to develop the self-confidence to build
the inner circle team before he jumps in to become a
digital entrepreneur.

We have discussed the simple, step-by-step architecting
and constructing of your life, with the integrated career
development method and the framework of career vision
and career development. Through growth and applying
an iterative process, it will enable you to create multiple
career options for a sustainable career choice, for long-term
growth.

Limiting self-belief: I am an experienced
professional in software engineering, and I
don't have business skills. If I get my
MBA, then I can become a business consultant, and
maybe my career will be successful.

Reality: In the digital era, the TSP, with the
requirement of dual competency for functional
experience, and information technology knowledge,
and skills like software programming or even business
software, is a great way to achieve success.

DUAL COMPETENCY =
FUNCTIONAL EXPERIENCE +
IT/DIGITAL SKILLS EXPERIENCE

From my working experience with many professionals in industries, and based on significant research, I found that using the TSP—talent stacking platform—with **dual deep competency**, led to success in the new digital era. Industries and organizations are already evolving and disrupting, and opening new career opportunities. There is a big digital skills gap, technically and functionally, of competency skills and subject matter experts. In functional experience with digital skills, both are required; it's like specialist expertise, with generalist knowledge. That will be the "mantra to success" in the next digital economy. If you have dual competency or industry expertise, with digital IT skills, this will be the key to success in the next digital economy, and will help you to architect your life, to accomplish your short-term objectives and long-term goals.

Talent Stack Platform (TSP):

The **Talent Stack Platform (TSP)** has multiple names; some people call it generalist or horizontal skills, or EEE—education, experience, and exposure. In the past years, we have always seen many people that want to become specialized early, to have an advantage compared to others. Some people, from childhood, decided to a take a unidirectional path, and have been very successful. Recent research shows that this is due to technology advancement, uncertainty, and automation. Specialized jobs are at risk, being taken over by either computers, robots, or machines, as machines and robots can work in a more accurate and predictable way. Machines learn and self-correct to improve performance. The talent stacking platform, for you, has multiple skills stacked together, of education, experience, and all kinds of exposure as horizontal skills development. Before you get to be a specialist, you will have multiple options to choose for your long-term job-scale, career-scale, and dream-scale, on your TSP; and as you grow, you can consistently develop vertical skills. The research only shows this for jobs, but even in sports or very specialized sports, there is an edge and an advantage for those who are specialized. It is important to use the TSP to choose and grow your skills.

5.1 TALENT STACK PLATFORM:

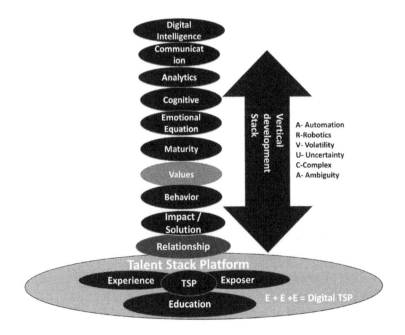

A "TSP"- talent stack platform is a very unique requirement for all age groups. Based on research, we have clarified 3 main categories of TSP and building based on your horizontal stack:

Category-1 – Ages 6 to 12: Early-Life Scale – Talent Stack Platform

Category-2 – Ages 22 to 28: Mid-Career Scale – Talent Stack Platform

Category-3 – Ages 50 to 60: High-Dream Scale – Talent Stack Platform

What is something in common between 20-time grand slam champion, Roger Federer; best-ever Indian cricket captain, Mr. Cool, MS Dhoni; and two-time NBA MVP champion, Steve Nash?

All three of them have been the greatest ever in their sports, and they all became specialized later in their careers. Roger Federer sampled a wide talent stack of sports before focusing on tennis in his early teens. Nash grew up playing soccer, and did not start playing until he was 13. And MS Dhoni was a man of many sports before choosing to play cricket. All of these elites were devoted earlier on in their deliberate practice of the activities on which they would eventually want to focus and become experts. Instead, they all underwent what researchers called a "talent stack platform," and what David Epstein called a "sampling period," in his new book, *Range*. They played a variety of sports, usually in an unstructured or lightly-structured environment, and they gained a range of physical proficiencies from which they could draw. They learned about their own abilities and proclivities, and they later decided to focus on and ramp up technical practice in one area. These basic principles are more relevant to sports, engineering, science, research, or information systems, etc. Whether you choose sports, engineering, science, or business, the category-1 TSP, for ages 6 to 12, is an opportunity to make a multi-disciplinary talent stack platform so that you have an option to choose whichever specialization you would like. The category-2 TSP, for ages 22 to 28, plays a key role in choosing a professional job or career-scale. There is the option to choose a specialty, which is key to build a foundation to success. The category-3 TSP, for ages 50 to 60, is where you are looking to shape up your dream-scale to accomplish your desired dream. See the table below as an example for reference, and ask what your TSP is

TABLE 5.1 TSP-TALENT STACKING PLATFORM TABLE REFERENCE

Category-1 Ages 6 to 12 Focus area examples:	Category-2 Ages 22 to 28 Focus area examples:	Category-3 Ages 50 to 60 Focus area examples:
Communication 1. Oral 2. Listening 3. Reading 4. Writing	Technical with **dual deep competency**	360-degree CHFFRFAP focus
Analytical skills	Problems and solutions	Dream-scale

Category-1 Ages 6 to 12 Focus area examples:	Category-2 Ages 22 to 28 Focus area examples:	Category-3 Ages 50 to 60 Focus area examples:
Personal, emotional, & social development	Cross geo knowledge and intellectual	Give back to society
Knowledge & understanding of the world	Horizontal skills	Fun-Focus run for life or charity
Creative development	Vertical development	Create for next generation
Physical development	CHFFRFAP	Dream clarity

On top of your TSP, with your education, experience, and exposure, you can develop vertical development skills, and acquire continued improvement to scale up. These vertical stacks are relationship, impact, behavior, values, maturity, emotional equitation, cognitive, analytics, communication and digital intelligence, and equation.

EMPOWER YOURSELF WITH MULTIPLE CAREER CHOICES, BUT ONE AT A TIME

In today's digital economy, the best way to architect your future is to have multiple options that are functional, technical, or even artistic. I am going to ask you to choose at least three key competencies: one short term, for 2 to 3 years, which gives immediate results; and two to three, for

5 to 15 years, in case the first one does not exist, or for any reason is displaced due to the advancement of technology or the economy. It should be a long-term dream view, with a dual competency (**dual deep competency**) way to architecting your future.

In the case that you have an artistic mindset, and you are looking at sales, marketing, HR, or even personal administration, then you should be looking at option B, for technology skills, software programming, digital marketing, or robotic automation and workflow, or even apply artificial intelligence to use Chatbot or Cabot, etc., as an alternative.

Simply, when you are planning to look for two options, option A and B are totally different approaches: One could be technical, and the other could be functional, as an artist, adventurer, writer, actor, or even a digipreneur.

As an example, see the diagram below, which can help you to apply it to your career/job, finances, and healthcare.

5.2 DUAL DEEP COMPETENCY:

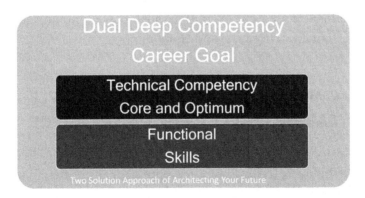

Sample Questions: " What Do I want to be when I grow up ?" or what kind of job I want to be when I graduate ? or what kind of life I want to be after my retirements ?

These three are just an example, but you can choose as many as you like, to focus and build a career strategy, and to create a blueprint. We call it your *life* ***career adventure plan*** (CAP). In case one does not work, then you can fall back to Plan B, with dual competency and a totally different plan than your first one. In the case that you are a technical or scientific person, then you could look for totally different skills, such as marketing, banking, HR, sales, manufacturing, or even in the arts or in sports, or in SMEs or in languages, such as an English, French, Japanese, or Hindi language translator, or for any foreign language. Subject matter experts will always have an option. Finally, the third option would be your long-term dream view, which may take 5 to 10 years, or even 15 years. For example, a business entrepreneur or social entrepreneur, or subject matter researchers or independent consultants.

Please refer to the career adventure plan (CAP) below, for reference and a workbook.

You may be asking why the short term is 2 to 3 years, and not 6 months to 12 months; And why the long term is about 5 to 10 years, and not 15 to 20 years.

In today's digital and fast-moving economy, technology disruption and changes are happening too fast, so 3 to 5 years would be too long, and there would be major changes in industries; so 2 to 3 years would be a good enough time to consider and upgrade your skills in order to enable yourself to move forward. If you take more time to acquire new skills, you may see yourself being outdated and obsolete.

I have interviewed and researched more than 100 of my students and colleagues, and my finding is that architecting your future, with dual competency and a dual career plan, makes you more successful in today's digital economy, and in the future. You can start to have multiple options and grow in your career, because your requirements will change, as the demand for skills and knowledge is changing frequently. No matter which stage you are at in your life, you may start with plan A and grow, but in comparison, developing a plan B as an alternative career option, and an option C, as long-term enjoyable goals, will help toward your long-term career plan and your dream view.

The best option to architect your life is to design your choice.

Why should you design your choices and have options to consider?

How can someone have multiple choices in their career?

When should you consider multiple options?

Option-A: Is what you are currently working on. Your first plan is what you have in your mind or are currently pursuing or expanding as a career idea. This is the activity that is making you a living. It requires your attention to continue.

Option-B: Is what you will choose when option-A does not work as per your plan, and you need to depend on an alternative. Option-A is not supporting your career growth, and is not having the desired result you were expecting.

Options-C: Is that thing you would like to do on your dream-scale, where money or your self-image is of no concern or worry; especially if you know that you could live your life better, and it makes sense, you enjoy doing it, and you can see that it makes a difference in others' lives.

We all have a lot of lives within us, and we surely live more than two or three different lives in particular moments. Of course, we can live one at a time to fully enjoy a meaningful life, but we would like to ideate multiple options and choices in order to be future-proof.

Designing your choices is to have multiple competency and options. You can plan and give yourself choices, when you are doing very well in your life or even during uncertainty. You can master and pick up alternative skills any time to adopt and grow. We call it dual competency skills. It's not a combination of choices that complement each other it's identical choices. As early as you choose, you can compound the benefits.

 Limiting self-belief: I am working in the healthcare industry as a doctor, and it is difficult to change my industry.

Reality: You can have multiple ways to live your life, and it's never too late to change your domain. When choosing to combine healthcare with technology, it's a unique combination of industries.

MAKING THE RIGHT CHOICE

Dil Maange More!!!!

(This is a Hindi quote, which means: This heart desires more.) Always keep your desire high to have better choices in life...

Architecting your future and your life requires not only that you have lots of options and choices, as we have discussed, but also that you have more options for growth and happiness.

Everyone wants to be happy; we want to be happy, and we want our friends, students, and colleagues to be happy and joyful. The secret to being happy in a life of architecting your future is not about "making the right choice;" it's about learning to choose, and living every moment of your decision.

You can do all the work of architecting your life—understanding your purpose, exploring your "why" and ideating, developing multiple tools and alternatives, and implementing them—but this doesn't mean that you have made the right choice, or that you will get what you desire and be happy. Maybe you will end up happy and getting what you want, and maybe you won't. We say *maybe*, because being happy, and thinking about getting what you want, are not about future opportunities, risks, or unknowns, or whether you are picking the right options; it's about how you choose, and about how much you commit, and you live with your choice once it is made. All of your hard work and effort is undone by your poor choosing. But even if you make the wrong choice—yes, that is a risk, but truly, not a big one—you can revert back. Accepting, adopting, and understanding a good, smart, healthy, and financially-friendly life design process and method is critical to a better outcome. It is seen in work, job, and career models that are chosen, where people cut themselves off from their most important insights, and it actually prevents them from being happy and joyful with the choice they have made, and they don't follow up. Many people guarantee an unhappy outcome by how they approach things, and this is all important when architecting your future steps to make the right choice.

On the flipside, the right choice will almost always guarantee a happy and positive life outcome, while setting up for more options and the promise of a great future.

"You have two choices; you can make a living or you can design a life."

—Jim Rohn

APPROACH YOUR CHOICE BY ARCHITECTURAL THINKING METHODOLOGY:

The best way to architecting your future is to work on the processes that we had discussed to apply the UEDIC framework for the integrated career development method.

UEDIC is as follows:

U = Understanding
E= Exploring
D= Developing
I = Implementing
C= Confirming

5.3 UDEIC MODEL:

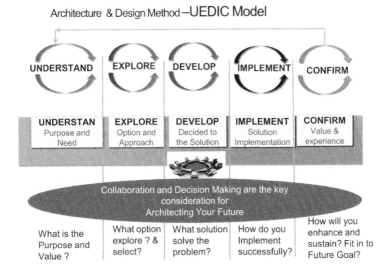

Architecture & Design Method –UEDIC Model

In choosing to architect your life, the process has 5 steps: You have to understand your purpose and values; ideate and explore possible options; develop and narrow down a few options; implement; and finally, confirm. In case option number one doesn't work, then re-create an alternative option, and follow the steps till you get confirmation, but don't agonize over it too much—if you find that something does not work, look for an alternative and move on.

We need to understand each of the steps to appreciate the important difference between positive choosing which are happy outcomes and future prospects and negative choosing, which are unhappy outcomes.

Step-1 UNDERSTAND: To understand is the best way to know your purpose before you start doing something, and we have been discussing this throughout this book.

Do an assessment of yourself in every area—job, career, health, wealth, and art and play and decide where you need improvement, set up your goal accordingly, and accomplish it. Write down your job/work view, career view, and dream view, which are required to be aligned with each other, and to make your life meaningful in the short and long term.

Step-2 EXPLORE: Exploring is about having good insight about yourself. You need to explore your options for your short and long-term choices and alternatives. Some people think that they don't have many options; others think that they have too many. The most important thing is where and how you get engaged with your inner circle, and how you create proof of value (POV) with your outer world, defining the prototype of your possible solution, ideating, and reaching out to get an expert's opinion, who has done similar work in the past. Explore how he or she is an expert, and how they live their day-to-day life, and then make a collective decision: Is this my interest, and is this the life I want live? An architect always has too many options to choose from, but the real decisions are based on ideation, the best possible outcome, and most importantly, on looking forward to the future, and at purpose and requirements. From here, he can clearly drive the outcome and integrate it with the end result, which is called the dream view of your life. If you have few options, then you should get more people's advice and input so that you can invest more time to cultivate better and suitable ideas, to make your future better. After all, it's your life, and you are the *architect of your future.*

Knowing this requires that you educate and grow your awareness, by controlling your breath and the oxygen flow to your brain and body, in an emotional, spiritual, and intuitive way. The most commonly affirmed way to such maturity has been personal and group practice, such as a journaling, prayer, spiritual exercises, meditation, and integrated physical and mental practice, like yoga, Asana, tai-chi, and many more.

Step-3 DEVELOP: This is about decisions. You decide and choose what is best for you and your future. You finally get down to making a choice from your narrowed-down list of alternatives, and you have cognitively evaluated the issues, and have emotionally, mentally, and spiritually contemplated the alternatives.

In summary, exploring and developing ideas and steps are as follows:

- **Idea-1 Connect the dots for job view, life view, and dream view.**
- **Idea-2 Think about the problem and the solutions.**
- **Idea-3 Have a 1 to 3-year, and a 5 to 10-year career adventure plan (CAP plan).**
- **Idea-4 Ideate and prototype your choice, to minimize the options.**
- **Idea-5 Choosing well is the key for development and execution.**

The key to exploring and reframing your ideas for options is to realize that if you have too many options, you actually have none at all. If you are daunting yourself, and you feel stuck, or can't get in front of your possible options list, then you don't in fact have any options. Please remember that options create value in your life when they are chosen correctly and are realized. You get paid for how much value you bring to the market place.

To be more valuable, choosing well is the key, and we need to understand how our brains work in the process of choosing through either feeling, thinking, or emotions. Where do good choices come from, and how do you know if you have chosen well? We are now living in an era of intelligence and unprecedented progress in the research of the brain and the human power of emotional intelligence.

The *New York Times* science writer, Dan Goldman, in 1995, wrote about his idea about emotional intelligence, and a cultural phenomenon was launched. *Emotional intelligence* is something everyone understands and follows to learn. Another way to make choices is based on cognitive knowing, by learning effective forms of intuition, spirituality, and knowing.

Step-4 IMPLEMENT: Basic actions, taken in regard to your decisions, are implemented step by step for execution. Now you are required to grow and start working on developing not thinking back but only focusing on what you want to become. Assume that you have discussed, ideated, and finally come up with three options as a final outcome for the decisions you need to develop. For development, you need to start with option-A, and when selected, you think, eat, breath, exercise, and deep dive to drive only option-A. You have chosen, and you become a single-focused person, but then you see a ray of success you know what I mean to drive crazily toward your chosen success of one path, option-A. You then try to apply what you have chosen to option-B, and similarly to apply it to option-C, as these are all your best alternatives for your careers. You become a master of the skills and subjects you have chosen as your options. This architectural thinking approach and process is about experiencing who you would most like to be. This technique and method is not guaranteed (There is no quick solution.), but you can see your intention to reach a solution via alternative options, by making logical, emotional, spiritual, social, and intuitive decisions. You have chosen, and you can rely on it.

Step-5 CONFIRM: Confirming is the key to remembering that imagined choices don't really exist, because many times they're not actionable. We are not trying to architect your fantasy future life, but a real, actionable, and livable life. You know and try to look comfortable with everything about your decision, which of course you should do if you're going to confirm. We revel in exploring a few possibilities, and then take action by making choices and building our way forward. If it is not actionable, then you can move on.

So let's get better and better at building, by getting better and better at letting go of the options we don't need any longer, and having the confidence to know that we can get more options in the future. This is the key to making the right choice, and confirming and being happy with the choice.

When in doubt, let go and move forward...

It's really simple.

I am not saying that you should pretend you don't know about your career path and roads not taken, or that you will never again discover something halfway down the path and decide to back up and make a correction... In the architectural thinking process, you always have to be looking backward and forward, and whenever it is required, you need to iterate and change. That is the smart way to proceed, which will be significant in enhancing your ability to be successful, and in implementing your choice, which will lead to happiness and satisfaction in your journey.

Take the example of Abhinav's: He is 14 years old and is from India. He has completed an HSC and wants to become a life sciences researcher, as this is a very specialized domain. We now need to find out why he wants to do this.

What is Abhinav's purpose?

Is it passion?

Is it understanding? Or is it his future promise?

How can he build his path forward?

And in his case, can his parents help to support him, as he is a teenager and may not have a perspective on his future.

The same process and support can apply to imagining being Superman, Batman, a doctor or an engineer, a movie maker, a poet, or even a writer, singer, dancer, etc...

**Architectural Thinking + Design Thinking =
Architecting Your Future**

5.4 ARCHITECTURAL THINKING APPROACH:

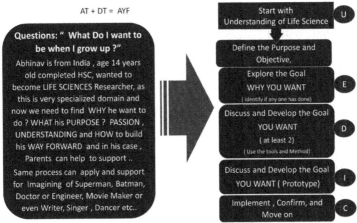

5.5 ARCHITECTURAL THINKING APPROACH
(Abhinav's example)

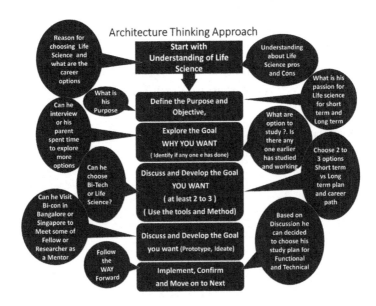

In summary, Abhinav's future desire is to become a life science researcher, and he has applied the *architecting your future integrated method* to understand, explore, develop, implement, and confirm the step-by-step process to decide how to go about his study plan, and what the way forward is for his future.

 Limiting self-belief: Architecture and design thinking are the same process, and it is hard to apply this for life designing.

Reality: There are many methods to apply, but architects visualize the future by applying clear understanding, exploring options, deciding the best ideating with prototyping, and taking action to move on. There is no right or wrong option; it depends on the individual, and it may or may not work for everyone.

GETTING THINGS DONE

Architects don't agonize. They have a clear vision, and apply architectural thinking for the future. They don't dream about what could have been. They don't waste their future by hoping for a better past. Architects see design in whatever life they are currently building and living in. This is how you choose happiness, and how you future-proof the architecting of your life, to realize your future.

Quick Summary

Architecting your live make your more valuable and rare, and accumulate and build your talent stack platform of experience, exposure, and skills; but when you feel like you have enough, go deep into your interest, and develop **dual deep competency** for the long term. Roger Federer and MS Dhoni may have changed sports when they were young, but they eventually decided to master the game of tennis and cricket. If you apply your five steps UEDIC methodology to choice your one career and grow with dual deep career competency.

I love the recent scientific sports research that was presented by David Epstein.

> *"When you have doubts, and you feel like you're falling behind your peers, fear not,"* Epstein says. *"One study showed that early career specializers jumped out to an earnings lead after college, but that later specializers made up for the head start by finding work that better fit their skills and personalities."*
>
> *"We learn who we are in practice, not in theory."*
>
> **– David Epstein**

EXPLORING ACTIVITY 5.1: Architecture Your Lives

1. Write down all your career goals, and purpose for your life, for 1–3 years, 3–5 years, and 5–10 years.

2. Choose your option-A, option-B, and option-C for your career, health, and finances; identify your primary function skills and knowledge required, and how you can apply digital and IT skills and have double competency. And if you are a technically or scientifically skilled person, then apply function skills, and see how you can apply this to have double competency, aligned with a long-term dream view.

3. Based on your option-A, B, and C, identify your peer, mentor, or coach who has done the same in the past, or has lived a similar life. Discuss his point of view (POV), and see if you like his way of living life and you are willing to commit your architecting your future live.

4. Research and apply your option-A, B, and C, with *U-understand, E-Explore and Ideate, D-Discuss and Develop, I-Implement with Prototype,* and finally, C-Confirm to take your decision forward.

5. Define your U:_____
6. Explore your E:_____
7. Discuss with Mentor or Coach:_____
8. Implement with prototype: _____
9. Confirm if you like to proceed:_____

MOTIVATE
"We will strive to comprehend what
will make us achieve our goals by
understanding what the driving forces
ARE, which will convert our thoughts
into behaviors and, ultimately, results.
More specifically, they will try
to predict how..."

CHAPTER 6

What Motivates You To Achieve Your Goals

How could I write a guide to setting and achieving goals if I didn't actually give you a few tips on the most important part of setting goals? The key to successful goal setting is your ability to motivate yourself, keep the momentum, and stay motivated until you have achieved your goals.

> *"Strength does not come from physical capacity. It comes from an indomitable will."*
>
> —**Mahatma Gandhi**

Limiting self-belief: I can only enjoy myself when I have achieved my goal.

Reality: Your goal is one of the milestones. When you enjoy your journey to achieving your goal, then you will have more fulfillment and fun, and you will be able to manage all aspects of your life. Make your goal a learning journey so that you can continue to progress.

Getting and staying motivated is not as difficult as it may seem. It just takes discipline and self-commitment. Let's look at the thing that you should do in order to get and stay motivated.

First, let's take a look at what motivation really is. Motivation is not a product of outside influence; it is a natural product of your desire to achieve something, and your belief that you are capable of doing it. Positive goals that are geared toward your pleasure are much more powerful motivators than negative ones that are based on fear. The right combination of both are the most powerful and motivating mix for goals.

Now let's look at what you can actually do to motivate yourself and stay tuned that way.

1. Start with visualizing your future success realistically, and model the feelings you'll experience when you achieve it.

2. Mentally (inner self-talk) walk the path toward this success, and base your feelings on different milestones on the way... I found that what is most powerful is your self-talk; it makes you stronger, and you think more positively if you feel and see promises from your goals.

3. Assign a high priority and purpose to each task that you must achieve, which will give each task a priority in your mind. (Keep only a few priorities; keeping 3 is Multi-dimensional disorder the most ideal case.)

4. Set a target for the amount of work you will do each day toward your goals. (Keep minimum time, commit to start, and build the habits;

research shows that if you do something for 26 weeks consistently, it becomes part of your integral life, and you form the habits.)

5. Visualize the desired outcome: Create a picture of what the desired outcome will look like, and have this vision in your mind at all times.

6. Set milestones of the things you like to do, the things that you are good at, and enjoy it.

7. Use visual indicators to monitor progress, and complete the task.

8. Give yourself affirmations to remind yourself how capable you are of reaching your goals.

9. Watch movies that motivate you.

10. Listen to music that motivates you, and practice mindfulness yoga. I have found that regular practice of mindfulness works like magic daily, especially with heart breathing.

11. If you work better with competition, make a deal with a friend or family member to compete for the goal, to see who gets there first! It can be hypothetical and doesn't necessarily have to be for real.

12. Get help and support from people around you, or from a professional in the field; for example, a personal trainer, finance manager, etc.

13. Define your own version of success; don't let others define success for you.

14. Ignore any negative influences or responses to your efforts.

15. Make a conscious effort to do better than you have ever done in the past, to keep motivation high.

16. Focus on the positive achievements that boost your positive emotions, and not the negative ones.

17. Share your successes with others, as this will keep you focused and will help you voice your accomplishments, which will realize your achievements for you.

18. Acknowledge your strengths and weaknesses, and work on them to analyze and improve.

19. Train yourself to finish what you start by refusing to quit until you are done.

20. Don't be afraid to make mistakes, and don't punish yourself for making them if you do.

Quick Summary

In this motivational chapter, we have discussed how to keep your goals, which can motivate you and make you feel that you can do more and more, and that you can achieve them. This has a lot to do with your mindset. We all get excited to start a big goal, we make big plans and, after a few weeks, we are back to zero. There are various reasons, but if you are realistic, and you analyze and define your goal, with a strong reason to do it or not to do it, then its purpose is simplified. Motivation plays a vital role to make your goal a success, and to stay and stick with your plan on purpose. Motivation is not what you like to do; it's your inner voice.

Let's see how to set goals in your life:

How to get whatever you want: ASK. The art of asking is important. Asking is the beginning of receiving; receiving is not a problem, and it's automatic. Receiving is like the ocean, so ask for more... don't ask for a teaspoon of the ocean.

Two ways to ask: 1) Ask with intelligence (when, how, and what). 2) Ask with faith (believe that you will get).

So, "Make plans like an adult, and believe like a child." It's the most incredible way to make it happen.

 ## EXPLORING ACTIVITY 6.1:
Motivation and Momentum

1. Write down all factors that make you motivated and bring you into the flow of enjoyment.

2. Write down all purposeful goals, and a timeline that you have in your mind to achieve your goals.

3. Write down the support required to achieve your goal, and how you will celebrate after achieving your goal, and with whom.

 "Technology is a gift of god. After the gift of life, it is perhaps the greatest of god's gifts. It is the mother of civilizations, of arts and sciences."

—Freeman Dyson

Energy Leads To Performance – Time Vs Energy Vs Focus

CHAPTER 7

Time management is not a new subject, and this is a top topic for every person. Everyone is busy in this digital economy because everyone has a mobile device at hand, and they are accessible to everyone in the world. Effective time management and goal setting begins and ends with self-management, as time is limited (24 hours, or 1,440 minutes, or 86,400 seconds) in a day. We must be able to balance between time and energy, and focus in the best possible way in order to achieve our goals by producing the results, which is called productivity. Productivity depends on us, and how we are managing ourselves. Most of us fail to achieve goals because we lack self-management, energy, time, and focus.

That is why this section needed to be included in this book, to show you how to be productive and how to do more in less time, so that you don't have to manage time but rather your outcomes and results. The concept of time management has been in existence for more than 100 years, believe it or not. Unfortunately, the term, *time management*, creates a false impression of what a person is able to do and what his priority is. Time can't be managed; time is uncontrollable, and we can only manage ourselves and our use of energy and focus. That is all that can be done. Time management is actually about self-management. For effective time management, we need to balance the energy and have the ability to plan, delegate, organize, and focus on a direction, and control every aspect of our lives just to find 30 minutes a day that is devoted and focused on something productive that is just for us. We can call it a focus funnel on our priorities. You can either do each task now, or eliminate, automate, delegate, or procrastinate on purpose to re-prioritize, so that you get to see the results and outcomes. Rather than looking at time and worrying about the day, pre-planning accomplishes your goal.

Limiting self-belief: I am busy with my work, and I do not have enough time to keep up with learning new things.

Reality: Productivity means managing your energy on the scale of time, with focus.

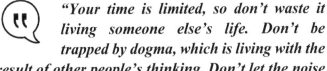

"Your time is limited, so don't waste it living someone else's life. Don't be trapped by dogma, which is living with the result of other people's thinking. Don't let the noise of others' opinions drown out your own inner voice. And most important, have the courage to follow your heart and intuition."

—Steve Jobs

7.1 PRODUCTIVITY MODEL

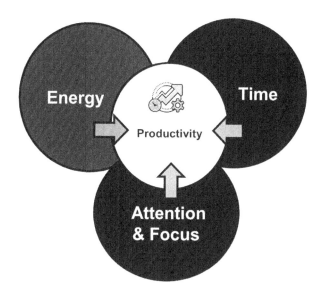

7.2 FOCUS FUNNEL

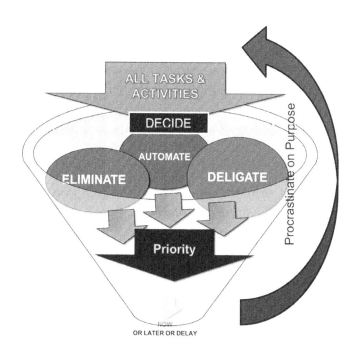

Why Does Productivity Matter in Digital Destruction, Especially Now?

You always need to ask what the key objective of productivity is, to make self-management better.

Primary reasons due to two major considerations:

- **Get more time to do more things in your life.**

- **Spend time on the right thing, to make it more meaningful to yourself and your family.**

If you want to do more things in your life, and be successful, you need to architect your future, and spend your time wisely, as you are not going to be any younger than you are now. Always strive to be more valuable, so that you become wiser in your life.

Limiting self-belief: I don't have enough time to manage my health and fitness.

Reality: Time management is both an art and a science. Before managing your time, you need to control and manage your energy and attention, and focus with commitment to achieve your daily, weekly, monthly, and annual goals successfully.

There are common time wasters, which you need to identify in order to be productive:

In order for a self-management process to work, it is important to know what aspects of our personal and professional management need to be improved. Otherwise, what is the point in trying?

Below, you will find some of the most common reasons for reducing effectiveness in and around our lives. You might want to check the ones that are causing the major obstacles for your own time and energy management. These are referred to as your time stealers.

PRODUCTIVITY PROCESS TO INDENTIFY

Identifying your time stealers: Who kills your productivity?

- Interruptions – for example, the telephone or TV (These are also distractions.)
- Interruptions – for example, guests, WhatsApp, Facebook, Social media etc.
- Unwanted meetings or passive meetings
- Tasks you should have had someone else do for you
- Procrastination and indecision
- Acting without total information
- Dealing with other people's issues or problems
- Some sort of personal crisis – for example, family member is sick or injured
- Unclear communication
- Inadequate knowledge
- Unclear objectives and priorities
- Lack of planning
- Stress, anxiety, and fatigue

- Inability to say "No" to anybody with a request
- Personal disorganization

There are quite a few, aren't there? Fortunately, there are strategies you can use to manage your time in a better way, and to be more in control and reduce stress, but you can analyze your time and see how you may be both the cause and the solution to your time challenges.

Below, we will look at time and self-management issues in more detail, to ask yourself:

1. **Shifting priorities and crisis management.** Management guru, Peter Drucker, says that "crisis management is actually the form of management preferred by most managers." What is ironic is that actions taken before the crisis could have prevented it in the first place.

2. **Lack of priorities/objectives.** This is probably the biggest and most important time waster. It affects all we do, both professionally and personally. Those who accomplish the most in a day know exactly what they want to accomplish beforehand—just ask Donald Trump.

   Unfortunately, too many of us think that goals and objectives are yearly things and not daily considerations. This results in too much time spent on the minor things, and not enough on the things that are important to our lives.

3. **Attempting too much.** Many people today feel that they have to accomplish everything yesterday, and don't give themselves enough

time to do things properly. This only leads to half-finished projects and no feeling of achievement, as all things are done in a hurry and appear rushed to others.

4. **Meeting and greeting visitors.** The five deadliest words that rob your time are "Have you got a minute?" Everyone does it: colleagues, the boss, your peers, and your family and friends. Knowing how to deal with interruptions is one of the best skills you can learn.

5. **Ineffective delegation.** Good delegation is considered a key skill in both managers and leaders of homes and work. The best managers have an ability to delegate work to staff and family members to ensure that it is done correctly. This is probably the best way of building a team's moral, and reducing your own workload at the same time. The general rule is this: If one of your people around you can do it 80% as well as you can, then delegate it.

6. **Procrastination in purpose.** The biggest thief of time is not decision making but decision avoidance. By reducing the amount of procrastinating you do, you can substantially increase the amount of active time available to you.

7. **The inability to say "no."** The general rule is that if people can dump their work or problems onto your shoulders, they will do it. Some of the most stressed people around lack the skill to "just say no," for fear of upsetting people. Get over it, because these people can do it for you.

8. **Meetings.** Studies have shown that the average professional person spends about 17 hours a week in meetings, about 6 hours on the planning time, and untold hours on the follow-up. There are many ways we can manage our time. I have listed some strategies you can use to manage your time in a better and more efficient manner.

9. **The telephone.** Have you ever had one of those days when you just had to answer the phone with, "Grand Central Station, how can I help you?" The telephone can be your greatest communication tool, but it can also be your biggest enemy to effectiveness if you don't know how to control its hold over you.

They are noted below.

1. Always define your goals as clearly and concise as possible.

Do you find you are not doing what you want to do just because your goals have not been set properly yet? One of the factors that make successful and happy people stand out is their ability to work out what they want to achieve, and have written goals that they can review constantly. Your long-term goals should impact on your daily activities, and be included on your to-do list. Without a goal or objective, people tend to just drift off, personally and professionally.

2. Analyze your use of time.

Are you spending enough time on projects that may not be urgent now but are things that you need to do to develop yourself or your career?

If you are constantly asking yourself, "What can I do to make things easier for me right now?" it will help you to focus on *important* tasks, and stop reacting to tasks that seem urgent (or pleasant to do) but carry no importance toward your goals.

Try getting and using a personal calendar, and setting reminders on your computer, cell phone, or palm pilot.

3. Have a your own plan.

How can you achieve your goals without a plan? I don't even think that is possible.

Most people know what they want but have no plan to achieve it except by sheer hard work. What's the point in doing hard work when you don't know how to apply it?

Your yearly plan should be reviewed daily, and reset as your achievements are met. Successful people make lists constantly.

It enables them to stay on top of priorities and remain flexible to changing priorities. This should be done for both personal and business goals.

4. Action plan analysis.

Problems will always happen when you set a plan. The value of a good plan is to identify them early and seek out solutions immediately. Positive energy and time management enables you to measure the progress toward your goals, because "What you can measure, you can control."

Always try to be proactive in the achievement of successfully managing your time, with self-management. Time management is not a hard subject to understand, but unless you are committed to building better self-management techniques into your daily routine, you'll only achieve partial (or no) results, and end up right back where you started. You have to commit to managing your time and self-management better, and remember to include time for yourself. The lesson that you need to learn is that the more time you spend planning your time and activities, the more time you will have for those activities. By setting goals and eliminating time wasters, and doing this every day, you may find you will have extra time in the week to spend on those people and activities most important to you and your family.

Five Steps Productive Principle:

Productivity can be measured by the activity you accomplish in your daily life. Based on research, if you concentrate on three to four major activities in a day, one at a time, you can produce more results than you would if you were to have more activities, where you wouldn't accomplish as much (as expressed in the graph below, to analyze and for your reference).

7.3 PRODUCTIVITY ON PURPOSE (POP) GRAPHS

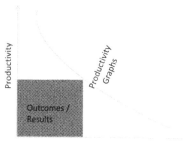

Productivity on Purpose and Priority

How to calculate daily productivity
Total earning in $ / 2000 hrs
Example : $100,000/2000 hrs
= 500$/hrs
You need generate at least 500$ of worth per hours of outcome for your to be productive.

So acquire the skills which matter to you for productivity on purpose.
Develop the skills 1,2, 3 to be more valuable to you ..

The vertical line in the POP graph indicates the productivity on purpose, and the horizontal line indicates the activities you can achieve in a day. The maximum meaningful activities that you can do with focus and achieve them, is three.

Rule-1 – Identify 3 things you want to accomplish in Day/Month/Year

Rule-2 – One thing at a time, apply the productivity on purpose.

Rule-3 – Cultivate your energy. (Bring yourself into a positive (+ve) mindset, with positive emotions.)

Rule-4 – Disconnect from all distractions (email, internet, non-value added activities that are not on your priority list) till you have accomplished your important tasks every day.

Rule-5 – Stop day dreaming, and control, focus, and drive toward outcomes.

All the above are techniques for you to support and manage your life better, and to be happy by architecting your future to achieve your life goals for your life and your dream-scale.

Quick Summary

Time management is not a new subject; it has been going on for more than 100 years. I am sure that most of you have read or heard about the successful book, *The 7 Habits of Highly Effective People*, by Stephen Covey. Today, everyone has challenges, and every 2nd person you ask, you get the response, "I don't have time." Everyone has the same 24 hours in a day, but you have to manage your energy, focus, and attention; and self-management becomes a key to success, and leads from the inside in the distracting digital era. We have gone over some of the best possible ways to lead and create productivity models, identify time wasters and time stealers, and create productivity on purpose.

EXPLORING ACTIVITY 7.1: Time, Energy, Focus, Self-Management – 3G-3F-30M Rules (3 Goals, 3 Focuses, and 30-Minute Priority)

1. Write down all your priority and purpose goals for your life as they relate to your life-scale, career-scale and dream-scale, for which you consider life to be happy and joyful.

2. Write down all your goals, with a timeline and the support required to achieve the goals.

3. Write down the support required to achieve your goals, and how you will celebrate after achieving them.

Energy, Physiology, Stress For Goal Achievement

E nergy directly links with your performance, and is highly driven by your behavior, observation of stress, positive thinking, and happiness in your daily routine in life. Management doesn't seem like something that would be a part of setting goals, but it could be the difference between you achieving them and not achieving them, along with tracking your progress. The source of energy and performance is stress.

> **Limiting self-belief:** My stress level is very high, and I can't manage it.
>
> **Reality:** In the digital economy, with a disruptive environment, everyone has stress; even primary school kids have stress today, due to homework, class work, and video/mobile games. If you take it positively, and have an awareness of the impact, then you will be able to manage it, with positive energy.

There are two levels: positive stress and negative stress. Positive stress adds anticipation and excitement to life, and we all thrive under a certain amount of stress. Deadlines, competitions, confrontations, and even our frustrations and sorrows add depth and enrichment to our lives. Our goal is not to eliminate stress but to learn how to manage it, and how to use it to help us achieve our goals. Insufficient stress acts as a depressant and may leave you feeling bored or dejected; on the other hand, excessive stress may leave you feeling all mixed up inside. You need to analyze and find the optimal level of stress that will individually motivate but not overwhelm you.

"Working hard for something we don't care about is called stress; working hard for something we love is called passion."

—Simon Sinek

Identifying Your Optimal Stress

There is no single level of stress that is optimal for every person. We are all individual creatures, with unique requirements. As such, what is distressing to one may be a joy to another. And even when we agree that a particular event is distressing, we are likely to differ in our physiological and psychological responses to it. That's just human nature.

The person who loves to arbitrate disputes, and moves from job site to job site, would be stressed in a job that was stable and routine, whereas the person who thrives under stable conditions would very likely be stressed on a job where duties were highly varied. Also, our personal stress requirements, and the amount that we can tolerate before we become distressed, changes with age. It has been found that most illnesses are related to unrelieved stress; for example, anxiety disorders, bowel disorders, etc.

This is best described by Viktor Frankl, Holocaust survivor: *"Between stimulus and response, there is a space. In that space is our power to choose our response. In our response lies our growth and our freedom."*

If you are experiencing symptoms of stress, you have gone beyond your optimal stress level; you need to reduce the stress in your life, and/or improve your ability to manage it.

Some basic stress symptoms are included below for better understanding, but are not limited to:

- Hair falling out
- Anxiety attacks
- Headaches
- Fatigue
- Loss of appetite
- Increased appetite
- Depression, etc..

Can You Manage Your Stress Better?

Identifying unrelieved stress, and being aware of its effect on our lives, is not sufficient for reducing its harmful effects. Just as there are many sources of stress, there are many possibilities for its management as well.

However, all require work in order to be effective. Action needs to be taken for changing the source of stress, and/or for changing your reaction to it. You might be wondering how you are going to do this. Let me show you.

Become aware of your stressors, and your emotional and physical reactions:

- Notice your stress and its beginnings. Don't ignore it. Don't gloss over your problems.
- Determine what events stress you out. How much do these events mean to you?
- Determine how your body responds to the stress. Do you become nervous or physically upset? If so, in what specific ways?

Recognize what you can change:

- Can you change your stressors by avoiding or eliminating them completely?
- Can you reduce their intensity over time?
- Can you shorten your exposure to stress by taking a break or leaving the physical premises?
- Can you devote the time and energy necessary to making a change? (Goal setting, energy and time management techniques, and delayed gratification strategies may be helpful here.)

Reduce the intensity of your emotional reactions to stress:

The stress reaction is triggered by your perception of danger and/or fears, physical danger or emotional danger, and fears of failure, etc.

- Are you viewing your stressors in exaggerated terms, and/or taking a difficult situation and making it a disaster?

- Are you expecting to please everyone because I'm telling you that you can't?

- Are you overreacting and viewing things as absolutely critical and urgent all the time? Do you feel you must always come out the winner in every situation?

- Work at adopting more moderate views; try to see the stress as something you can cope with rather than something that overpowers you.

- Try to temper your excess emotions. Put the situation in perspective. Do not labor on the negative aspects of everything; find a positive in them if you can.

- Take personal time to evaluate your surroundings clearly.

- Take a deep breath when overly stressed, and count backwards from 10.

- Exercise a little bit or take a walk daily.

230 Architecting Your Future

Build your physical reserves:

- Eat well-balanced, nutritious meals.
- Maintain your ideal weight or appearance.
- Avoid nicotine, excessive caffeine, and alcohol.
- Mix leisure with work. Take breaks and get away when you can.
- Get enough sleep. Be as consistent with your sleep schedule as possible.

Maintain your emotional reserves:

- Develop some mutually supportive friendships/ relationships.
- Pursue realistic goals that are meaningful to you, rather than goals that others have for you that you do not share, because they won't succeed.
- Expect some frustrations, failures, and sorrows, and let them go.
- Always be kind and gentle with yourself; be your own best friend.

Quick Summary

In this chapter, we have discussed our energy and physiology links with stress management. Identifying stress, and management, is key to successful goal setting and achieving it. We have discussed how to mitigate stress and convert it into positive energy, and the key concept of reducing the intensity of your emotional reactions to stress management.

EXPLORING ACTIVITY 8.1: Managing Energy and Emotion for Performance

1. Write down all activities that will make you happy and interested to learn.

2. Identify your stress-creating activity, and discuss it with your mentor or coach, if you have one; or share your problem and seek honest opinions from someone who is the subject matter expert in that area.

3. Once you identify the root cause of stress, create your routine table, and take small steps toward resolving it.

Your Inner Circle Of Influence

CHAPTER 9

Architecting your future inner circle is not just about connecting with people but keeping the quality of your relationship with key team members, who will either influence you or be influenced and supported, reminding you from time to time how you are doing. Your inner circle relationship can help to build and architect your future, to make it an integral part of your success. The research has proven that a successful relationship with your inner circle not only makes you more successful but also makes you happier and more energetic, which is the secret behind why architecting, designing, and building together makes your life project a success. Architects are always supported by ideas, trust, and connection and collaboration with various people, processes, technology, and thoughts. You can't have a life with meaningful successes without your digital inner circle being complete. When you apply an architectural thinking process to design your life, you are virtually creating an imaginary goal, and are getting support from your parents, family, friends, colleagues, teachers, mentors, coaches, and community. The life design is all about your life and living with other people's efforts and hard work to make you successful. That is why I say that architecting your future is a team game, and everyone plays a key role to make you successful. When we talk about inner circles, it's all about gathering the requirements, defining the vision, associating and collaborating with others, and working together to make small projects as big as you want, with the influence and proof of concepts to find a suitable solution. And it can't be done alone. We have identified and explained three major influencers for your inner circle, which require tight integration to work together to drive your short-term objective and long-term goal, to make life meaningful.

9.1 INTELLECTUAL INNER CIRCLE:

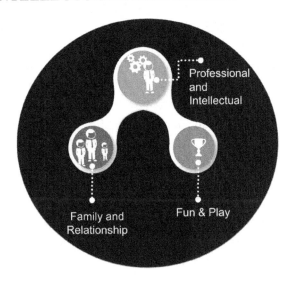

As you can see, the circle of your digital inner circle has been divided into 3 major areas: I) professional and intellectual, II) fun and play, III) family and relationship. All these inner circles are equally important, but the quality of your trusted circle is more important than the quantity.

- Your **professional and intellectual** inner circle plays a very intuitive role in your life. It starts from any age. Research has shown that if you have a strong growth mindset of a golden inner circle, you learn and grow 3 times more than others who don't have a strong and trusted inner circle. Sometimes we forget that it is important for us to keep up a like-minded inner circle in our personal and professional lives. To continue growing and building in the new digital economy, we are required to keep developing new friendships for new learning, and for learning from each other. Thanks to today's social technology that has been created, we have a platform we can use to be in touch and collaborate seamlessly with anyone, in any part of the world. LinkedIn and Skype are great examples of platforms that allow us to connect digitally to anyone, anywhere in the world; but it depends on the individual and how good and trustworthy their inner circle is, in order to be established and grow.

- The **fun and play** inner circle gives your life meaning and makes life fun. Whether you are a sports person, an artist, a musician, or a video gamer, keeping a "fun and play" inner circle keeps you motivated. This creates interest and motivation to keep up your learning and to have fun. With the same common interests, and skills, learning, and social support, we can help the world converge together, to influence or be an influencer in the world, which is a unique way to grow.

- The **family and relationship** inner circle is the foundation of any circle, to start to build and grow equally in order to support your inner circle, to be successful in your life. Study and research proves that good relationships keep us happier and healthier. There are three big relationship lessons. The first is that social connections are really good for us, and being lonely never allows us to grow. It also turns out that people who are more socially connected to family, friends, and community are happier and physically healthier, and they live longer. And we know that you can still be lonely in a crowd, or in a marriage, but you can still build strong relationships. The second lesson is that family relationships are not about how many connections we have with each other, but it is the quality and trust of those connected relationships that is important. Living in the midst of good, warm relationships is protective. Good relationships not only protect our bodies; they also protect our minds and our brains. It turns out that by being in securely attached relationships in your old age, you can count on being sharper and living longer.

A well architectured life can be built with strong and healthier relationships in your digital inner circle.

IDENTIFYING AND PREPARING YOUR INNER CIRCLE

9.2 INNER CIRCLE TOWER:

Digital intellectual Inner Circle - current status and then you know how to build the Digital Inner Circle for Architecure your future.

The inner circle of influence is divided into four sections. Each section has significance as we grow in our lives:

- Academic and education
- Professional
- Fun and play
- Family

Before preparing your team, you need to understand that architecting means that you need to own the responsibility, as it's your career and your future prospects. You need to be very clear on your responsibility and ownership, and that your team is there to support you, and they are there to consult with when you seek an opinion. Preparing your digital team means that everyone is engaging and participating in architecting your future, but everyone plays a different role in making you a success. In my professional days of working, most of the time, we need to interact with internal stakeholders, external stake holders, clients, peers, partners, and other eco-systems. We call it the TEAM role and responsibility support structure. It really works very well in professional careers, and it is the same thing that you need to apply in your personal career, because you are co-creating your future. Many people have already done this in the past, and you can surely learn from their struggling, failures, successes, and recommendations. Please see the definitions below; you need to identify each of your members as part of your inner circle.

9.3 TEAM CIRCLE:

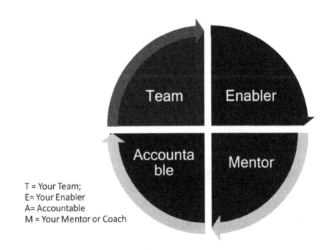

T = Your Team;
E= Your Enabler
A= Accountable
M = Your Mentor or Coach

Team: The team is your internal stakeholder for your inner circle, with whom you engage and work on architecting your future program. You will be working for the short term and the long term as a key member, to share and interact with each other on regular intervals. The candidate from your team with whom you have the most trust, you can invite to support your adventure journey, and you can add value and ideas, and have feedback sessions for your career adventure plan (CAP).

Enabler: Enablers include all kinds of supporters, subject matter experts, counsellors, and advisers, who can provide the encouragement to keep you going forward. Most enablers are your friends, but remember that not all friends are enablers for you. How many enablers you have primarily depends on your personality, attitude, thinking, and mindset, and what you believe that enabler can do for you. Your enabler range should be from 3 to 5 people maximum, who can be active participants and support you in your journey. When you are a team player kind of person, you can easily get more than you can expect as support.

Accountable: Being accountable plays a key role in architecting your future, as you are responsible for everything in your life and what you want from your team, enabler, or/and mentor. You are not only accountable, but you're responsible, and responsibility comes with ownership. As this book is all about you—WORK HARD ON YOUR JOB, HARDER ON YOURSELF, AND HARDEST ON YOUR FUTURE—ultimately, you are accountable for your career adventure plan (CAP) journey.

Mentor: Mentors play a very key and special role nowadays for architecting your future. Mentorship engagement is a new concept, which we mostly use for our job, work, and career development, or even for a new hiring process. Identifying a good mentor is key, and it should be aligned with your studies, job, career, and dream view. You must try to find out and participate in mentorship for architecting your life for the future. I have greatly used and definitely recommend having a mentor; it has provided me with the best outcomes in my life.

A mentor can also provide you with significant benefits, with regular guidance and accountability for your success.

Can a mentor also act as an adviser or counsellor for your life?

Good advice and recommendations come from people who have indisputable expertise. You can seek advice from doctors, tax consultants, or insurance advisers, but there is no expert advice for architecting your future. Everyone has their individual lives, but you are the architect, and you are responsible for architecting your future path and game plan.

Many people ask me for advice—friends, people from colleges, and colleagues from various organizations on LinkedIn—and I always recommend and can provide counselling.

Counselling is entirely different, and it is always helpful. You can get clarity, and a grasp of one's own best wisdom and insights. Explore this with someone who can provide you counselling, for clarity and a more settled and mature state of mind, which is an asset to you. This is where a good mentor plays the part of a master, and I would say that the best legitimate mentoring is centered on counselling.

How can you find a master mentor?

In today's digital era, it is very easy to identify your mentor, which will help you elevate your professional career growth, and have support when you need it. The greatest example today is LinkedIn, where you can identify respective mentors based on your profile and your requirements for architecting your future plan.

YOUR PROTOCOL WITH
YOUR INNER CIRCLE

The objective of setting up your inner circle needs to be kept simple, and based on outcomes so that everyone gets benefits. Your inner circle is your key focus to support you in architecting your future. Your inner circle is your co-creation of the future of your life design, and their role should be to provide a facilitator for ideation, intellectual discussion, the future of the workforce, and new skills, either vertical or horizontal. The facilitator usually should be you, as you are architecting your future, and you are driving the idea and creating for yourself so that you can be sure that the team is on track, and that your inner circle is enough to get the best outcome for architecting your life. You may delegate other inner-circle members to facilitate and drive conversation in the meeting. The important point is to have an inner circle to focus on keeping on point in regard to your time, agenda, and conversation relevant to architecting your life.

It is most important for the conversation to be on-topic, about your future and your design for life. Your inner circle should provide a facilitator, as well as active participants that will do research based on your topics; and everyone should listen and contribute to architecting your future. The ideal way to organize is through face-to-face meetings, but if your inner circle is in different cities, countries, and regions, then you would have to organize by way of a live video conference, with live discussion. And finally, it should be:

1. Objective-driven for career, job, and professional development.
2. Inner circle respectful.
3. Actively participative, making it creative and fun.
4. Idea generating, with positive constructing and thinking, and not skeptical or judging, with unnecessary criticism of the inner circle or topics.

BUILDING YOUR DIGITAL COMMUNITY:

This includes your internal stakeholders, external stakeholders, clients, partners, and other eco-systems. We call this your circle of digital community, with responsibility. Since the world has become much smaller than expected, our communication and community has become more common. We use Facebook, WebEx, Skype, WeChat, WhatsApp, and LinkedIn, with many more multiple technical and social forums available. They keep our communities alive.

Quick Summary

In this chapter, we have discussed: a) why we need an inner circle; b) golden inner circle, and how to build one; c) your TEAM (team, enabler, accountable, mentor) to guide you throughout your journey, which is your inner circle for career, job, professional, health, and finance; d) how to maintain it and become an influencer with common protocol. Today, due to technology, the world has become a single and common media platform. Because of tools and global communities, it is easy to communicate and collaborate, and to maintain your inner circle.

EXPLORING ACTIVITY 9.1:
Build Your Inner Circle for
Transforming Your Future

Build your inner circle for transforming your future (with dual competency DC-OT-OS-OF-2L: one technology, one specialty, one function, and two language for architecting your future in digital era).

1. Why is your inner circle important for you?

2. Assess yourself for each circle, and write how you can improve from your current stage to your future stage.

3. Identify your inner circle team as in "TEAM."

    1. Team member 2. Enabler 3.Accountable
    4. Mentors

4. Identify what your strength is as an influencer, and how you can lead your life established on your digital inner circle for architecting your life.

5. Create your own digital inner circle mind-map that is aligned with your job, career, life, and dream views.

Can Technology Help Heal the World?

Technology does not create prosperity, but people do. A digipreneur is a digital human, technologically empowered to create prosperity in the new digital era.

MORE FREEDOM:

"It is one of humanity's most ancient fantasies that someday we can all have our material needs fulfilled without drudgery, freeing us to pursue our true interests, amusements, or passions. And that someday, no one will have to toil at an unpleasant task, because food, clothing, and shelter, and all other basics for living, will be provided by automatized servants that do all our biddings."

**– Andrew McAfee,
MIT scientist and researcher in digital technology**

Get Digital, Get Hired

W e are heading toward the most challenging territory of the future, called the digital era. Technology has decreased the demand for low-skilled information workers, but it has increased it for highly skilled and knowledgeable workers globally. Requirements have been added to the new "digital human," to enable them to learn digital technology and become a digipreneur—a creative, social, and emotional champion.

A digipreneur is a digital human, who has to become a digital entrepreneur in order to empower digital prosperity skills with an entrepreneur mindset, in the new Information Age. To become a competent digital leader, you need three dimensional skills to be successful.

10.1 DUAL DEEP COMPETENCY WITH GROWTH MINDSET

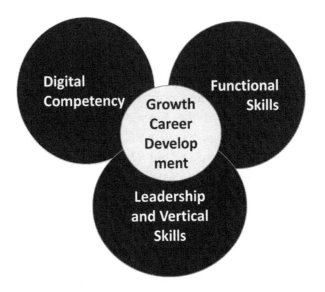

Thus far, we have seen how architecting your future is required in order to discover and assess yourself, set up personal and professional development goals, transition into the new digital era, and create and map your success. These are essential for personal development, but the real reason is to keep up with the innovation and digitization, because industries and organizations are disrupting and transforming. As you can see, technology continues to disrupt the industries and organizations, and that influences our careers and jobs to be disrupted. Let's look at the trends in industry transformation in the digital world, which are creating new value, steadily migrating to digital transformation, and giving the digital entrepreneur (digipreneur) an opportunity to find new prospects and careers.

Limiting self-belief: Technology will bring prosperity, wealth, and growth for the future.

Reality: Technology does not create prosperity, but people do, with technology. Digital humans will create prosperity, wealth, and growth in the information age.

The trend and pattern that we often hear is that we are living in uniquely disruptive times, and technology is accelerating the industries. The first half of the 20th century was also a remarkable period, featuring many important innovations. If we compare the two eras, we can surely think it is indisputable that the last 50 years of information technology does not come close to matching either the social or economic impact of the 50 years before that.

We are not saying this to disparage the advances of our time, but to make more important the Industrial Revolution. Every generation faces and is forced to keep up this challenge. Consider what the biggest societal changes were: Physical postal mail to email, telephone to Skype live video, or telegram to telephone? Cars to self-driven cars, or horses to cars? Aircraft to drones, or ground to air transportation? Passive grids to smart grids, or the electrical grid itself? As endlessly fascinating as the Internet is today, radio, television, movies, and recorded music had as much revolutionary impact on our information and entertainment habits as Facebook, Twitter, Instagram, Netflix, Spotify, Telepresence, Wi-Fi, Virtual personal assistant, YouTube, and TED.

We are still in the very early and middle stages of this

game, and this book makes you understand what is trending, and the next one or two decades may well see advances that make today's economy seem primitive, as the work of information and science communities invent and re-invent virtually every organization, industry, and human. The future is for digital human entrepreneur's digipreneur that design everything.

A digipreneur requires horizontal skills, along with vertical development and deep learning, which cannot easily be replicable by machine, robot, automation, or AI/VR.

Today, we are already living with the technology of automation, robotics, volatility, analytics, uncertainty, and a complex and ambiguous lifestyle.

10.2 TSP WITH HORIZONTAL SKILLS AND VERTICAL DEVELOPLMENT:

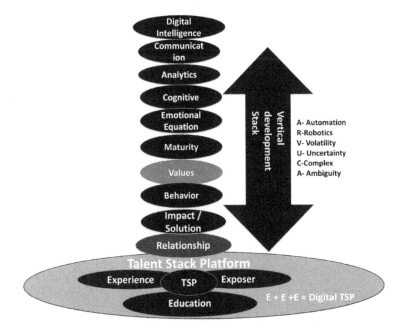

Horizontal skills are education, exposure, and experience. These are stacked with foundation skills to develop your vertical development, like relationship, impact, value, maturity, cognitive, analytic, and communication, in the digital era, to be successful. Talent stacking platforms get developed in the areas of experience and exposure. Education is a foundation, experience is knowledge, and exposure is like giving back your experience to the larger community.

Is the digital era a fear or a fact for human life, for now and in the future?

There has always been the fear that computers, automation, robots, analytics, and machine learning and intelligence would eventually lead to human diminishment or even obsolescence. These old and new concerns are now being expressed more regularly and more urgently than ever, even by some technologists in recent times, such as Elon Musk, who has proven technology's innovation and change, and the impact of the digital era. These warnings and messages fall under the following main categories:

- **Economic impact:** There is much discussion of the likely extent of job losses due to machine intelligence, artificial intelligence, and automation. The effects on economic inequality, and the subsequent need for a "guaranteed income," has been a major highlight in recent times, and a debate in some countries.

- **Diminished human capital and worth:** If machines integrate with digital technology, will they turn out to be better than humans at just about everything? And how will this affect our sense of ourselves? What can we look for in the future?

- **Ethics:** There is much debate about algorithmic biases and manipulation, fake news, digital currency, and in particular, how driverless cars and robots should behave in no-win situations and controversies.

- **Technology innovation:** Technology will continue innovating to sustain and keep up with micro and macro economies. Technology innovation is part of every industry, whether it is sports, education, entertainment, research, banking and finance, retail, healthcare, or manufacturing.

In today's digital era, it's hard to predict which organizations, industries, and vertical skills will survive for the next 5 to 10 years. Charles Darwin's quote reminds us to keep our heads up and look forward: *"It is not the strongest of the species that survive, nor the most intelligent, but those most able to change."*

As per research and history of the trend, and my observation over the last two decades, these fears and worries will prove to be exaggerated. This is the case so far, but in the current situation and the near future, the benefits of the combination of artificial intelligence (AI), machine intelligence (MI), robotics, automation (RA), the speed of the Internet, and human intelligence (HI) will be real, while the downside will remain almost entirely speculative.

In contrast, **Rob Reich**, Professor of Political Science at Stanford University, said, *"If the baseline for making a projection about the next today is the current level of benefit/*

harm of digital life, then I am willing to express a confident judgment that the next decade will bring a net harm to people's well-being. The massive and undeniable benefits of digital life—access to knowledge and culture—have been mostly realized. The harms have begun to come into view just over the past few years, and the trend line is moving consistently in a negative direction. I am mainly worried about corporate and governmental power to surveil users (attendant loss of privacy and security), about the degraded public sphere and its new corporate owners that care not much for sustaining democratic governance. And then there are the worries about AI [artificial intelligence] and the technological displacement of labor. And finally, the addictive technologies that have captured the attention and mind space of the youngest generation. All in all, digital life is now threatening our psychological, economic, and political well-being."

Anonymous research scientist and professor views:

The technologies that 50 years ago we could only dream of in science fiction novels, which we then actually created with so much faith and hope in their power to unite us and make us free, have been co-opted into tools of surveillance, behavioral manipulation, radicalization, and addiction.

However, we certainly can't rule out the possibility that this balance might shift over the long term, and thus the overall MI, AI, RA and HI debate will surely continue, and the future will have to be kept under a progress scanner.

Digital Trend, Disruption, and Future Path to Digital era

The digital trend and disruption is developing as a stake that serves as the central nervous system, which is the global technology companies globally, and is accelerating the industries' specific disruptions. It's dominant in the market for computers, new applications, software, Wi-Fi with 5G, software base gateway controllers, networking equipment, newer database technology, higher storage systems, system virtualization, operating systems, cloud technology and all kinds of new semiconductors.

 Limiting self-belief: I am doing very well in my life and may need to work hard in Technology arena.

Reality: You cannot do well in your life if you are not able to manage every aspect of your life with technology developments.

10.3 TECHNOLOGY AND INDUSTRY DISRUPTIONS:

Disruptions from Technology to Industries

Technology Disruptions	Industries-Specific Disruptions
- Cloud, SaaS, PaaS, IaaS	-Healthcare- Self-services, Doctor on demand, diagnoses, IOT
- Mobility, Apps	-Transportations; Shared, electric and self – drive
- Social media	
- Open Source, Open stack	- Banking; Digital banking, lending, block chain, Fin-tech
- BIG Data , Data Lake, and Analytics	
- Sensors, Wearable, IoT,	-Insurance; Personalized ,algorithmic
- Wi-Fi , Controller, Software define	- Manufacturing; Automation,Robatics,3D Printing , IOT
-Speech, Facial reorganization, IP-CCTV	
-Unified Video and conferencing	-Retail; Amazon, zero inventory,
- AR/VR/ED/AI/MI/ML	- Educations; Personalized, On-demand, Flip-Board , Spark
-Security, Cyber Security	
	-Legal; Smart contract, digital truth
	-Hotel / Hospitality: Airbnb,
	-City: Smart city and Smart campus ,Building

As you can see in the above diagram, both technology and industry are progressively disrupting globally. Initially, it was very US, Silicon Valley driven, but now we are seeing multiple mini-Silicon Valleys in China, India, Poland, and many smaller countries are becoming digital nation with venture capitalists, seed and angel investors in conjunction with small to large startups across the country and other regions in the world.

The left side is technology disruption, and the right side is industry disruption, which will bring the dual disruption opportunity to drive technology globally. Technology is one media to drive disruption, but human connectivity and agility brings acceleration to disruptions.

See the good example of how AI/MI and robotic automation processes impact on customer services and customer care for high volume processes.

This dual disruption will influence every company today that is being challenged by all forms of disruption due to consumer needs, and requirements are demanding, regulations are changing, and business conditions are changing. Product and collaboration of services are evolving at a rapid speed. As customer experience becomes more of a differentiator, there is tremendous change in the market related to MI, AI, and robotics. This includes a redesigning process so they can become streamlined to meet client's expectations of immediacy. This is not a new innovation. In the early 90s, when I used to work for one of largest, global, multi-national banks, interactive voice response(IVR) was introduced and integrated with CTI to provide banking clients the expectation and immediacy for better collaboration experience, and the results added a 300% faster response, high client satisfaction, and better cost optimization.

The next wave is the combination of robotic automation (RA) and AI, which gives organizations the ability to do more with less. MI, AI, and robotics are changing business models and augmenting worker productivity. Moving repetitive, high-volume tasks to a robot, delivers great benefits in efficiency, and workers are also now free to move into a role that requires more creativity and critical thinking.

Of course, all of this will provide choices in the human workforce, to be diverted to higher-value aims. MI/AI will bring the next wave of automation and productivity into business processes and customer interactions. The industries that will thrive in the future will see AI as not just a cost reduction, but rather as a way of redeploying people to drive a superior customer experience, and differentiate the organizations in their market strategies. MI, AI, and robotics, with other integrated technology, can be truly transformative.

Next, we will see how technological transitions and transformations are progressing:

The diagram below shows the disrupting curve of technology, and shows that industries grow as linear progressing growth, but when you apply newer technology, industries get exponential growth due to technology advancement and improvement, helping productivity and efficiency. This is the beauty of technology, which impacts industries as well as people, who are also empowered to get exponential growth. This has been the trend in the last 25 years since the Internet and web technology arrived.

But an interesting time is yet to come, for industry and technology advancement is on the way to disrupt industries, organizations, environments, and social and cultural improvements.

10.4 DISRUPTIVE CURVE OF TECHNOLOGY

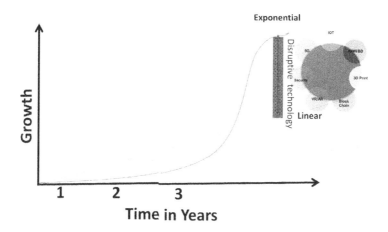

Research shows that software is disrupting the world, but I have a real question to ask!

Is software eating the world, or creating an opportunity for the world?

As you can see, the trend of software has been devouring the world since the early days of the Internet and the World Wide Web launch. You can find virtually everything, from credit cards to virtual offices, as the trend for a business. You can see, below, how all kinds of physical products have been converted into virtual products, and it has added a significant disruption and is going to continue in the digital era.

10.5 VIRTUAL DIGITAL ERA

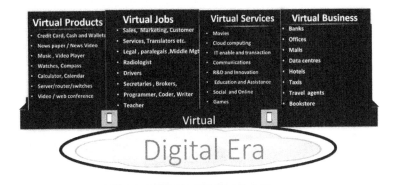

In all of the above uses, the software has been disrupting, and the software version is either free or less expensive than physical products, has better functions and quality, and is used and adopted globally. Smart phones are a really great example, which have disrupted products and their life cycle. You can see how many products are no longer required physically. In the current trend, the virtualization of cash, payment wallets, and credit and identity cards are certain to follow and get disrupted by software very soon, as environment and financial benefits are substantial and underappreciated. Software's ability to virtualize jobs and services is quite sensitive and debatable. Lastly, technology is also disrupting the physical office, mall, data centers, eBay, Ali express, and other e-commerce chains globally, and long-term societal effects will be profound. In summary, we are heading for a future of abundance, not scarcity, in the next technology and machine age. Humans are wired for leaner change, not necessarily for exponential change. Major transformation disruptions are happening in retail, and many physical stores have been closed or are in the process of being closed because of Amazon's, eBay, e-commerce's technology disruption and exponential change. The answer is to become a digital entrepreneur, and to learn the digital skills, with an entrepreneur development approach.

Today, exponential change is becoming a part of life, and science fiction is becoming a reality in our day-to-day lives. Take the example of food automation machines, where there is an automated agent to place your order and answer all your questions. There are robots used to greet you at your home and at hotels. There are driverless cars to drive you, drones to deliver your goods, and 3D printing to print 3D needs. Let technology lead us—institutions, organizations, and even our own mindsets—to increase learning, be prosperous, and support and grow.

Quick Summary

Technology is one of the major reasons for industrial transformation. Just a few years back, we thought globalization was creating a huge opportunity, but research shows that technology has over taken globalization and socialization both, and lead in the future of "globtech"- globalization with technological advancement. We have analyzed that technology disrupts the industries, and industries disrupt the people, and more is yet to come with robotics.

EXPLORING ACTIVITY 10.1: Digital Industries and Organizations

1. What industries do you think you like, and where do you see yourself in the next 5 or 10 years?

2. Identify the top 3 industries you like the most; research the trend of these Industries and how it will impact overall in the future.

   (Note: Keep in mind that today, there are 2 billion people under the age of 20.)

3. Identify 2 to 3 technologies that you have a personal interest in, and which you think will help to have an impact on your career, and boost your career Prospects and credibility.

   (Example: I have a personal interest in the banking industry and technology. I know that block chain and 5G/6G will be the technology of the future, to bring exponential growth in the future, even though it's not a widely accepted technology in many parts of the world).

   List your interests that you want to explore and learn in the next 2 to 3 years.

Digitize Your Career

CHAPTER 11

Economist Richard Baldwin believes past economics transformation indicate what the digitech future might hold. Historically, tech drives change. Its main challenge is to replace jobs lost to innovate with new jobs fast enough to ease social disruption. Thus far, we have seen how architecting your future requires you to set up personal and professional goals, and follow through to your map of success. As you can see, technology continues to disrupt industries and organizations, and provides an opportunity as well as forcing our careers to get disrupted. We have two choices: Either we wait and watch, or we be proactive to disrupt our future to be on the leading edge and lead above average. In the 21st century, in the digital machine era, every industry worker, at every level in today's ever-changing labor market, needs to be prepared with new skills in order to adapt and advance in the digital era workforce, to sustain and grow.

Limiting self-belief: I am not a digital kind of person, and I don't believe in digital social identity.

Reality: Today's digital social presence, facebook, twitter, email addresses are more important than physical presence and addresses. Whether you like it or not, the world is shifting toward the digital era. Digital intelligence (DQ) is becoming equally important as Emotional intelligence (EQ).

According to different workplace studies, more than 70 percent of employees said they are proactively learning new digital tools and skills to better adapt to digital change.

The diagram below represents how the digital era is transforming industries, and henceforth how individuals are required to transform with digital upskilling to match with industries' expectations, by digital skilling, collaboration, digital branding , dual competency skills, and following through with a digital entrepreneur architecture mindset.

11.1 DIGIPRENEUR MINDSET

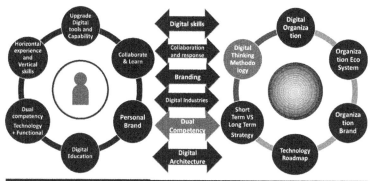

Digital Entrepreneur Mindsets (Digipreneur Mindset)

Digital Mindset Skills Developments Frame Work

For the alignment of the individual digital entrepreneur's mindset with the digital industry:

- Self-upgrading of digital tools, capability, and digital intelligence.

- Collaborate and learn new digital skills and knowledge.

- Creating personal digital branding is the key to success in the digital economy.

- Development of digital education mindsets.

- Dual competency = Digital competency + Functional competency (Example: information technology developer in healthcare; block chain with banking experience; digital marketing with client relationship management).

  This is just an example. I also recommend that you look at competency with sport or art/play as a 2nd competency, to make your career and life more exciting.

- Horizontal skills, like education, experience, and exposure, with vertical development, like connection, communication, and EQ/DQ, and analytical, cognitive, and critical problem solving skills, with a TSP approach.

Since you can see above that everything is getting disrupted by technology, individuals need to work on becoming digital humans by adopting digital skills.

I used to head the healthcare vertical for a global multinational company. Let me now explain and show you how digital technology will help healthcare professionals to disrupt the industries.

Medical communities use new technology to make advancements in everything from diet to science, to disease detection, to radiology. Adopted from Mr. Shapiro's forthcoming book, *Ninja Future: Secret of Success in the New World of Innovation*, here is how artificial intelligence, sensors, and even digital assistants like Amazon's Alexa, could help keep costs down and improve care.

Sensors and wearable devices will help doctors:

How do you respond when a doctor asks you to describe your health and your symptoms? Probably with a log of subjective, anecdotal self-analysis. And there is a gap between what is happening to your body and how you interpret it. The key to bridging this gap lies in wearable devices containing sensors, including micro-electromechanical systems, or MEMS. These tiny sensors activate in response to outside stimulus to detect change in location, air pressure, temperature, light, sound, and even smell. Consider a medical consultation powered by these sensors. Without asking a single question, your doctor could chart your physical activity and check your hydration, sodium, and oxygen levels without using a needle.

When AI is becoming a lifesaver:

Another example of AI is how it can be a lifesaver with the help of MEMS. Individual patients are generating millions of data points every day, but doctors and hospitals aren't able to view and understand this enormous volume of information. AI with MI can quickly sift through vast amounts of data to enhance caregiving, and even save lives. AI and MI is a game changer in healthcare because of its uncanny ability to identify patterns. That skill, searching for signs of abnormalities, is at the core of what pathologists do every day. Many startup based in the Asia, USA, UK, has created an AI + MI diagnostic system that claims to detect lung cancer in patients earlier than doctors can. And a team at Stanford University built a database of 130,000 skin disease images, and created an algorithm to diagnose skin cancer.

Another example of how IoT will benefit sensors:

Rick Phelps, founder of the online Alzheimer's and dementia support group, Memory People, was diagnosed with early-onset Alzheimer's. He had this to say about

Amazon's Alexa: "It has afforded me something that I have lost: memory. I can ask Alexa anything, and I get the answer instantly." In addition to acting as a cognitive crutch, AI-powered smart phone technology monitoring can monitor for falls and provide daily reminders for people with less severe memory loss. The Israeli startup, Intuition Robotics, has created ELLiQ, a robot for seniors, which can send reminders about appointments, message family and friends, respond to voice commands, and turn on music.

All the above show that environments are changing, and industries are changing, so careers and jobs are changing too. To keep up with technology disruption, we need to evolve our skills, education, and expertise with technology and functions.

Digitizing your career by monetization thinking:

Digitizing your career is best investment for "Architecting Your Future". Building your digital skills with digital mindset investment give you a 10 times more return. If you invest in yourself. There are many positive aspects of investment in digitizing your career. You will leading for front and ahead with others. You will get recognized, your thinking will always have faster and curious mindset to be ahead and consider to be innovators. Your career advancement particularly in disruptive technology will help you to be a leader in particular domain or industries or vertical. In digital era the greatest advantage of digitizing your career is your talent, your skills and talent are globalized so it easy for you to monetize but you are part of global workforce and bigger completive community. You can monetize your set of skill and TSP-Talent stack platform in virtual environment.

Quick Summary

   Industries are getting disrupted by technology and the deployment of automation but our education system is still following the legacy system to build career paths. By researching and working with various industries, the recommended way forward is to digitize your career. Start thinking about how your future will be driven, by thinking with a digital entrepreneur mindset. Have a digital mindset by upgrading your tools, collaborating, being reasonable in response as industries advance, being a **fast and curious** learner, building your digital brand, educating yourself as a digital educator, and keeping a **dual deep competency** mindset and functional competency, with digital enabler skills. The digital skills development and mind-set will help to monetize your investment faster than any other invest in your life. Architecting your future is holistic view of your life, career and dream. Please do your DQ-Digital intelligence questions and answers to do your assessment, and plan your way forward to digitize your career.

EXPLORING ACTIVITY 11.1:
Digital Career (Digipreneur)

DQ-Digital intelligence to identify your digital behavior, activities, career, and skills required to become a digipreneur:

Rate yourself from 1 to 10 on the following (1 = very little; 10 = very strong):

Note: Answer these questions for a thoughtful evaluation and a means to become a digipreneur.

Your Score : _____   Your % Score _____

Questions 1 to 12: to analyze where you are and what actions are needed to plan for your future in digital era

Q-1: I believe that improving my digital competence and skills has become important for both me, my family, and my career.

Q-2: I believe that information sharing and collaboration is now an integral part of my day-to-day life.

Q-3: I regularly use Digital e-book reader, kindle, and google reader, blogger, to help inform and organize my life.

Q-4: Being much more open and transparent will be increasingly necessary in my work and personal life.

Q-5: I believe that success in the digital is just as important as in the physical world.

Q-6: I take my online image as seriously as my in-person style and appearance.

Q-7: I have thought through how I want to appear on LinkedIn, Twitter, Facebook, and Instagram.

Q-8: I understand that my personal networks of inner circle are an essential part of my overall identity.

Q-9: My approach to personal branding online is already giving me real personal and career advantages.

Q-10: Digital technology has caused me to rethink my life's priorities and the way I run my life for now and in the future.

Q-11: Information technology is improving the purpose of my work, personal family life, and my organization.

Q-12: Technology is an essential force for making a better world and a better future.

Scoring Grade:

A= 100 or higher: You are a digipreneur and clearly a leader with a digital mindset and the digital skills to navigate yourself to becoming a success in the digital era.

B= 65–80: You are a digipreneur and clearly a leader with a digital mindset and the digital skills to navigate your personal development.

C= 50–65: You are not a digipreneur, and you need to develop the digital technology leadership with a digital mindset and the digital skills to navigate for your personal development and growth.

D= 40–50: You will be struggling in the next 5 to 10 years; you need to develop the digital technology leadership with a digital mindset and the digital skills to navigate for your personal development, as well as keep your job or business.

E= 40 or under: You are in the danger zone, and you need to seek help from a digital consultant and a coach, or get digital skills development and education.

Confidential and Copyrighted

Seven Technology Disrupters For The Future

Now you have seen how to architecture your future by setting up your personal and professional goals, and following through to your map of success. As you can see, technology continues to impact our lives. Workers, at every level in today's ever-changing labor market, need to be prepared with skills to adapt and succeed in the new digital workplace and economy.

> **Limiting self-belief:** Software is eating current and future jobs.
>
> **Reality:** Technology advancement is part of industries' evaluations and globalization. We as humans have intelligence, and we need to prepare for the future. There will always be future opportunities and challenges.

The problem is, we continue living in an uncertain world, and because of the high levels of uncertainty we all face, people of all ages and career levels are finding it difficult to know what new skills to learn, what courses to take, and what degrees to get that will provide them with the most opportunity going forward. Uncertainty keeps us stuck in the present. Certainty, on the other hand, gives us the confidence to make a bold decision for the future, to move forward with confidence, and to invest time and money to learn new things. Over the past two decades have experience with the world's best industries leading organization and have developed a proven methodology to anticipate disruption and change before it happens, allowing you to find the confidence that certainty provides. This new science of certainty involves a scientific method of separating *hard trends* (trends that will happen) from *soft trends* (trends that might happen). This method is currently being used by many Fortune 100 companies, including Google, IBM, Microsoft, HPE ,Cisco, Deloitte, GE, KPMG, and DXC, to name a few, as well as new startups, to provide an accurate roadmap of the opportunities that are ahead.

That's why I called this book, Architecting Your Future, and why I'm now helping you to connect the dots on how the trends are driven by technology. The outline below will transform every career and job prospect in the future, and create new ones. By providing a predictive roadmap for anyone who wishes to increase their personal career relevancy in a digital world of disruptive and transformative change, you can make career and education decisions with confidence. The list highlights technologies that are now ready for the future and will continue to transform current and future careers, and the job market. As you read through the list, ask yourself how each one will help you to play a key role in your industry, your personal career path, and which direction you need to choose to go...

12.1 SEVEN FUTURE TECHNOLOGY DISRUPTERS

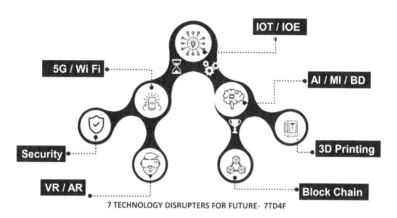

7 TECHNOLOGY DISRUPTERS FOR FUTURE- 7TD4F

Based on current and recent trends, not only is technology changing the world, but it is also creating the new world of the future, as well as bringing new promises. This is all interlinked technology, as well as interdependent, and a whole growth cycle for individuals and industries. I have captured high levels as a whole, but there are many layers of technology that will evolve and disrupt to grow and challenge the new technology. In a recent trend, cloud services and virtualization will be increasingly embraced by businesses of all sizes, as this represents a major shift in how organizations obtain and maintain software, hardware, services, and computing capacity. Information technology is rapidly becoming an on-demand service that is rapidly transforming all business processes and automation, resulting in a rapid evolution of current careers, as well as creating new opportunities for career advancement in functions and technology, both regionally and globally.

The 1st technology is:

- **IOT/IOE:** "Connecting everything" used to be buzz words and a puzzle a few years back. Now it is a reality to connect intelligent sensors with machines, using chips and micro sensors, and both wired and wireless networks will be creating a rapid growing Internet of things (IoT). The key benefits are the sharing of real-time data, performing diagnostics, and making remote connections. The IoT is already a big thing for industries, and will continue to grow, giving opportunities to many. This has been one of the biggest technology revolutions, and it is creating multiple paths for opportunities. Many jobs have been created by industry, as a whole, as we add intelligent, connected sensors to bridges, roads, buildings, homes, health and fitness centers, cars, cycle devices, and much more. In just a few years, there will be well over a billion machines talking to each other, and to people.

   The total projection for this industry is **\$318bn by 2023**, according to research submitted by Global Data, an analytics company, at a compounded annual growth rate (CAGR) of 20%. This means new industries, new jobs, and a better future in technology.

The 2nd technology:

- **AI & MI:** Artificial intelligence and machine intelligence are not new technologies, but its momentum is new. AI is the intelligence that is demonstrated by machines; therefore, it is called machine intelligence. AI is the system that can interpret any external data, learn from such, and can use the learning to complete the task and assigned goals. The key objective of AI is to implement the intelligence of humans in machines, by developing those that think, understand, learn, and behave in the same manner as humans. Machine learning, and intelligent e-personal assistants (Chatbots) using natural language voice commands, was launched with Apple's Siri, which was rapidly followed by Google, Microsoft, Amazon, and others, all offering what is rapidly evolving into a mobile electronic concierge on your phone, tablet, and television, gaining in the market faster than ever before.

Analytics empowered with machine intelligence describes the technologies and techniques used to capture and utilize the exponentially increasing streams of data, with the goal of bringing enterprise-wide visibility and insights to make rapid critical decisions by machine. This new level of data integration and analytics will require many new skills and cross-functional training in order to take advantage of new opportunities, as well as break down the many data and organizational silos that still exist, creating millions of job opportunities across the globe.

The technologies are rapidly evolving, and soon every profession, from retailers to maintenance workers, will have an Alexa-like assistant. Adding an e-personal assistant to support an existing product and/or service will create many new careers. My interaction and observation in Asia, particularly in Singapore, is that everything has been empowered and enabled by AI/MI—from post offices, to maps, to utilities, transport, to personal data, to tax. The new advancement with *advanced robotics and automation* is a giant leap forward, thanks to network sensors, artificial intelligence, and Amazon/Google/IBM voice communications, taking the next level of repetitive jobs from humans. At the same time, this is creating many new career opportunities, from design, programming, and installation, to service and maintenance, just to name a few, for knowledgeable, digital workers.

As I have been a technologist, and have got into the small, integral details and nuts and bolts of each technology in the past, and now am into the technology businesses of today, I know that you don't have to know the physics of a telephone in order to use it. Today's technology becomes so simple that you do have to know that it exists, and how to creatively use it to accomplish your goal, and to plan and explore. You don't have to wait until next year or the year after, or until you're laid off. Everything is available at your fingertips, to know everything. Invest the time to identify what you need to learn right away to be ahead, so that you will thrive, both now and in the architecting of your future, either in your current career or in a new one.

Based on research presented by fourweekmba, AI's current market revenue is 3.5 billion and is expected to reach $26.4 billion by 2023, at a compounded annual growth rate (CAGR) of 40%, when combined with AI + MI + natural language processing (NLP) and robotics automation.

Robotics will displaced or eliminate many white-collar jobs faster than replacement jobs can be created.

The 3rd technology:

- **3D PRINTING:** Printing with additive manufacturing (3D printing) is creating many new careers in manufacturing, as this revolutionary technology allows any size company to manufacture quickly, locally, and with far fewer costs. Additive manufacturing builds things by depositing material, typically plastic or metal, layer by layer, until the final product is finished. Examples of final products today include jewelry, iPhone cases, shoes, car dashboards, parts for jet engines, prosthetic limbs, and much more. The worldwide 3D printing market size was estimated at $9.9 billion in 2008, and is estimated to be $34.8 billion by 2024, with a compounded annual growth rate (CAGR) of 23.2%. There is a significant push and demand for customized products, and for a reduction in manufacturing costs, processes, and downtime. Governments are investing in 3D printing projects, which is expected to greatly boost technologies, enabling new career opportunities in the digital era. I was interviewing some early adopters of 3D manufacturing, and they shared that the current trend in 3D printing applications is shifting from prototypes to functional parts in various areas such as medical, automobile, toys, and consumer goods.

The 4th technology:

- **BLOCK CHAIN:** Block chain will be increasingly embraced by businesses of all sizes, as this represents a major shift in how organizations obtain and maintain software, hardware, and computing capacity. IT is rapidly becoming an on-demand service that is rapidly transforming all business processes, resulting in a rapid evolution of current careers, as well as creating new careers in every functional area for various industries. Block chain is an emerging technology that can radically improve banking, supply chains, healthcare, and other transaction networks, and can create new opportunities for innovation. Businesses contain many examples of networks of individuals and organizations that collaborate to create value and wealth. These networks work together in markets that exchange assets in the form of goods and services between the participants. The promise of technology provides the basis for a dynamic shared ledger that can be applied to save time when recording transactions between parties, remove costs associated with intermediaries, and reduce risks of fraud and tampering of data. This is creating new opportunities for potential jobs or new businesses. Research also shows that block chain may create significant prosperity in society due to secure data and protections. Research, done by **Statista,** forecasts that block chain technology's revenue will be $23.3 billion by

2023. The financial services sector has been one of the quickest to invest and leverage the block chain technology, with approximately 50 to 60% adoption coming from finance and banking industries.

The 5th technology:

- **VR/AR:** Augmented reality (AR) and virtual reality (VR) are simulated experiences that can be similar or completely different from the real world. The applications of VR can include entertainment (gaming) and educational purposes. To simulate a virtual reality experience, a VR headset or multi-projected environment must be used to generate realistic images, sounds, and other sensations that simulate a user's physical presence in a virtual environment. A person using the virtual reality equipment will be able to look around the artificial/simulated world, move around in it, and even interact with virtual features or items. Today, VR/AR has become increasingly mobile, playing a major role in direct and indirect job creation for gaming and education. Remote visual communication is rapidly evolving into a primary relationship-building tool for businesses of all sizes, as employees use smartphones, tablets, and laptops in combination with current enterprise-level video conferencing systems, combined with mobile conferencing apps, to communicate at new levels with customers, partners, and employees. Virtual reality (VR), augmented reality (AR), and AI enhanced simulations, coupled with the gamification of education, will create many new careers as corporations and educational institutions, at all levels, accelerate learning by using advanced simulations, VR, and skill-based learning systems that are self-diagnostic, interactive, game-like, and competitive, all focused on giving the user an immersive experience, thanks to a photorealistic 3D interface, etc. The increase in the penetration of smartphones and connected devices in various application sectors, and the development of gaming industries, has boosted the AR/VR market growth. One great example in Denmark, "Augmented Reality" ("AR") assists paramedics and firefighters at crime scenes. Using a smartphone or iPad, a first responder communicates with a remote crime scene investigators, who "draws" circle around objects onsite that no one should touch. Surgeons use AR in combat zones. Globally, the AR/VR market stood at $11.35 billion in 2017, but for the years from 2018 to 2025, it is expected to be at $571.42 billion, and is expecting a compounded annual growth rate (CAGR) of 63.3%, which is the highest across the consumer technology, and creates new opportunities for architecting your future.

The 6th technology:

- **Security:** Cybersecurity and forensics is the biggest potential market for future development. Cyber security consists of IAM, encryption, UTM, antivirus/antimalware, firewall, IDS/IPS, DR and DDoS mitigation, etc. As you can see, the growth plan of all technology security plays a most important role in the area of preventive and reaction security portfolios for the future. In security, careers will be growing rapidly as we become increasingly connected and dependent on computer systems and machines, using intelligent sensors connected to just about everything. Careers in data and information forensics will grow rapidly as the need to solve cybercrimes increases. Based on recent research done by MarketsandMarkets, it is forecast that the cyber security market will grow from \$152.71 billion in 2018, to \$248 billion by 2023, with a compounded annual growth margin (CAGR) of 10.2%. This is a high estimation, but cyber security is becoming more important than ever.

The 7th technology:

- **5G:** 5G will continue to grow and rapidly evolve, and will create many new career opportunities for everyone as all phones become smartphones, as wearable devices with Smart Advisor and capabilities expand, and as our primary computer and tablets continue to evolve as our laptop replacement continues. This new level of mobility will allow any size business to disrupt and transform how it markets, sells, communicates, collaborates, educates, trains, and innovates, and will expand from developed countries to developing countries, and from city to city.

But as of now, every day, all across the world, people still experience the same frustrating glitch with their mobile devices. A poor mobile experience has major challenges, and 5G brings a promise to the world that it will converge service providers and unify wireless at a leading edge level. As of now, much focus is on the edge; in 2019, more applications and data will be moved to the edge, potentially with a lot of disruption from 5G with the cloud model. As technology becomes embedded in everything and everywhere, growth is **estimated at 163 zettabytes by 2025,** and organizations and industries will manage applications and data differently to support 5G growth. The major and real benefits that you get from 5G are due to lower latency and unified device connectivity which help to create products and innovations in digital era. As we have discussed in all the above technology, connectivity plays a key role in making applications, users experience and technology dependent businesses successful.

The information technology industries with mobile service providers continue to build unified, pervasive, and smart intelligence that goes beyond the cloud to include edge computing, IoT, machine learning and intelligence, augmented reality/virtual reality, block chain, and more. In the latest and greatest digital trend, companies are building new ways to disrupt the industries, with many decentralized applications (DApps). DApps will potentially continue to disrupt the cloud model. Data centralization is becoming a primary design principle for new multi-agent systems in the world, creating potential industries, career transformations, and better architecting of your future.

In this context, it is most frequently local, and the ability to maximize the value of reaction time is local as well. Centralized data draws data together locally, and with the increased size of data graphs, so too come the analytics. As these analytics begin to drive intelligent actions, more data and actors are drawn into the local orbit and end user centric. The real goal is to put that intelligence and end users ever closer to the data. Therefore, we will see major shifts toward event-driven applications and server less architectures that allow very small, very specific applications to run in lightweight edge and small data environments, which could be the device in your pocket, your home camera, or car, etc., and on devices that are on your wrist, embedded in your arm, retrofitted to your desk, or outside your house on a pylon. And yes, the expectation has increased from 5G wireless that will change the data accumulation patterns in disruptive ways to individual industries.

Recent research, in 2019, done by globe Newswire, forecasts $277 billion by 2025, with an estimated compounded annual growth rate (CAGR) of 111%, from year 2019 to 2025, in two parallel tracks, one with SIM cellular and another with machine to machine (M2M) SIM connection.

Based on research, and being an experienced technologist for last 2 decade, all 7 of these technologies will make a huge difference in the future, and will support to build and architect your future in the long term if you invest our potential with these technologies.

Quick Summary

In this chapter, we have discussed primarily the 7 global technologies that I may think can disrupt industries, and which are relevant to bring results and focus across all industries. The 7 technologies that have been researched are the core leading technologies that will drive the future of industries. There are many followers of the technologies, but no one knows which technology will be the leader, or who are the followers will be, but based on three decades of technology trends, we can anticipate the future of technology, to build and architect your future in the digital era. These 7 technologies are the Internet of things, and the Internet of everything (IOT/IOE); artificial intelligence and machine intelligence; 3D printing; AR/VR; cyber security and security; block chain; and 5G. You need to choose one area to apply your methodology of "UEDIC"—understanding, exploring, developing, implementing, and confirming—to move forward and architect your future by becoming a digipreneur in the digital era.

EXPLORING ACTIVITY 12.1:
7 Technology Transformation

Technology transforms your future:

1. Write down all areas of technology that you think are most suitable for your career, while considering your current experience and expertise.

2. Write down why you think your chosen technology will change your career or make suitable in your life. What is it for you?

3. Identify the Subject matter expert either be a technologist or leadership or Management in your chosen technology. Interview and spend time with him/ her to learn how his day would be looks like in day, and how it would be suitable for you. Is that you desire to do.

4. Based on discussion, create your own mind map from your current state to future state ,that is aligned with technology, and see how you see yourself in success in long-term career path.

Conclusion

N ow is the best time to Architecting your future, "Future of Work" is here, it will be driven by technology, technology causes economic transformation, which create exponential growth an opportunity. For 1000 year's economics relied on land production for human sustenance and growth. The first steam engines appeared in the 1700s, three centuries of economics growth and innovation, machines eliminated many farming jobs while creating new job and opportunities, Rapid growth and significant innovation created for the special century 1870-1970 machine economy, which created next generation of chain reaction of innovation and new job opportunity. Since 1970 till date globalization and technology innovation created "glorious decades of computer and communications" era. Today's conversations began about the "Digital Disruption". "Digipreneur" and "Future of work. The computer chips and communication speed expended the services sector. Emerging economies such as China took over manufacturing and India took over services outputs. "Global technology is favoring people who work with their technical skill, minds and collaborate, rewarding those who work with their hearts" but not the uneducated or unskilled. Globalization with technology progressing together are transforming.

Architecting your future is both art and science a short-term goal is science; a long-term goal is art and the most interesting part is that we need to apply both in the digital era.

MIT researcher, Larry Lessig, says:

> *"The past always tries to control the creativity that builds up on it. Free societies enable the future by limiting this power of the past."*

Now, even though you have read this entire book, this is not the end of architecting your future journey, nor is it mine. This is not the finish line but as a starting journey.

Assessment- discovery

As an architect, you need to assess and discovery before you are plotting the future, and you are visualizing, realizing, and knowing and loving yourself, to be ready for the future. Constructing and motivating play sources of energy. I hope you will apply this new way of continued learning and discovering. Build the talent stack platform within you, set priorities for your purpose, set goals, and grow in your journey to make your life more meaningful. Now you have a method and a framework of " UEDIC " understanding, exploring, developing, implementing, and confirming to learn the skills that you will need in order to think, design, prototype, and achieve your future goals. All of the goals that you set for yourself should make you think, "What person must I become to accomplish my goal? And what truly matters to me in order to have

"4Self-CDEF" an ongoing adventure with architecting my future?"

"TSP"- Talent stack platform

I am sure these methods, tools, and insights will help you continue to evolve, grow, and expand your horizontal skills and vertical development to support your "TSP"-talent stack platform. With every step of your defining process, you are crafting a path that will keep sparking your visualization, and inspiring you to be motivated to have a brighter future and a more meaningful life-scale, career-scale and dream-scale. You can sense, feel, and think so much more now. Technology continues to disrupt industries and organizations, and provides an opportunity as well as forcing our careers to get disrupted. TSP way to continue developing multiple talent to be ahead personally and professionally.

"Digipreneur"- Digital with Entrepreneur

"Globtech"- global technology and "Digipreneur"-digital entrepreneur radically change the future of work and the way architecture your future.

Global freelancer skilled workers from Poland, USA, India, China, Philippines and Thailand performing white-collar work, such domains as accounting, programming, services, support , are fractions of a European or US workers. Freelancer work is exploding and along with non-English speaking country. For one example is; "upwork.com having a freelancer of 14 million skilled worker across 100 nations" and growing exponentially. You are now becoming much closer to seeing your future in the digital era.

Dual Deep Competency

You are becoming more and more creative to learn for the future. A creative life is what an architect likes. A creative life is a life of new beginnings, and as you explore your visualization and digital entrepreneur skills, you will unlock new achievements and learning capabilities, and become a creative, digital person. Creativity becomes the stuff in your life so that you can compete with anyone and also plan an alternative to be a successor. It's how you think. It's what you see in front of you, what you visualize in your mind, and what is in your heart. It is how you express your feelings. It's how you make your life decisions. It's not just about what you create. What also matters is why you create to architect your future.

4SELF-CDEF

Your meaningful life-scale and your purpose, shaped by your values, and balanced by self-confidence with determination, self-realization and reflection, hunger to do well in your dream-scale, which serves as an evolving gravity of reference to pull you through the toughest moments, big or small, in your digital machine era. More than that, you will unlock digital experience and new opportunities you might not have otherwise thought of.

ELP

Energy link with performance-more energy, more money and more competency lead to more success. Energy always considered as a sources of inputs to provide positive thinking, feeling and behavior to build habit to support output as a performance. Physiology with ´emotion"-

electromagnetic motion in your physical body produce as a positive results to maintain your leadership energy.

Fast and Curious

IBM researcher has predicted that world information will be doubling in every 24 hours in near future. The **fast and curious**-learn faster to develop your skills and competency, be curious to get ahead in digital era. To build your inner circle for transforming your future recommend with dual competency "DC-OT-OS-OF-2L"- one technology, one specialty, one function, and two language for architecting your future in digital era.

Circle of Influence

Your circle of influencer and your Associations will lead to architecting your future either you get influenced or lets others get influenced by you. Positive association always pay you back and give you a positive results. **Two Major Laws to apply-**first is **"Life is like the seasons; it changes. If you want to get the benefits, you need to change".** 2nd law is ´ law of harvesting "you always reap what you sow… you always reap more than you sow". So investing holistically either in circle of influence or developing your digital skills and mindset both gives significant values and return.

Seven disruptive technology for transformative future

These technologies are the Internet of things, and the Internet of everything (IOT/IOE); artificial intelligence and machine intelligence; 3D printing; AR/VR; cyber security and security; block chain; and 5G. You need to apply your methodology of "UEDIC"—understanding, exploring, developing, implementing, and confirming—to move forward and architect your future by becoming a digipreneur in the digital era. In future Digitech and Digipreneur will less impact on job requiring an emotion, empathetic, physical presence, including farming, childcare, social care with touch and feel. Job that can "virtually" –approximately half of all technical, management, business, financial, support, research and development work can be done from anywhere. This is 30% of administrative jobs and 60% of jobs in higher skilled and professional, technical, scientific and advance analytical fields. Globtech may effect one in three US and Europe jobs.

"Cogitative, Artistic, social works and humanity jobs will be equally important in most in the "future of work" if you apply the technology in digital era.

Architecting Thinking for "AYF"-Architecting Your Future Manifesto

Hopefully, you have realized just how simple architecting your future and achieving your goals can be if you set your mind to having a successful future. Setting goals properly doesn't have to be the most difficult thing that you can do, because it can be very stimulating. If you build your manifesto, challenge yourself right, and set time aside to set your goals, you can and will complete them successfully. You have learned that procrastination is your enemy when you are trying to achieve something in your life, and you have learned that goals can be set for just about every aspect of your life, including family, relationships, finances, career, health/fitness, etc. Why should you waste your time dreaming and hoping for a better life when you can go and get one right now? You don't need to know anything other than what you have learned here, on your way to a better future. Get yourself on the right track, and start setting your goals today.

In summary, you have learned which can be applied every day to make your life more extraordinary and high performer in the digital era.

- How to clearly think about architecting your future, based on your current assessment and discovery model, to get your future direction.

- **Talent Stack Platform (TSP)**: Stack of horizontal skills, vertical development – generalist to specialist to legend.

- Goals: Prime motivation – Nothing happens without goals.

- **Dual Deep Competency**: Technology with functional skills to grow and resilient success for future.

- **Fast and Curious**: Learn faster, learn more and be more curious to get ahead in digital era.

- **ELP-Energy link with performance**-more energy, more money and more competency to lead more success.

- **Inner-Circle: Your circle of influencer and your associations**

- Digital Entrepreneur: Become a digital disrupter to lead in digital era.

- Seven global technology to disrupt the future and keep monetization in mind to take an advantage and advancement.

- Motivation and 4Self-CDEF: How to apply processes to motivate, energize, and personalize, and keep the flow of momentum.

AYF IN A PAGE SUMMARY

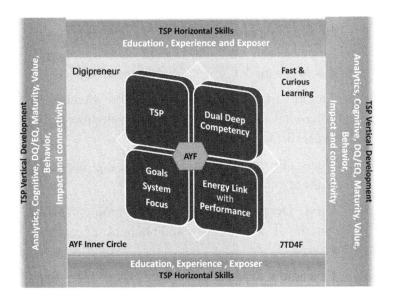

The Book That Got Written

This book could not have been written without the help of architectural thinking and learning during my working with IBM as an enterprise architect, in the early phase of my career. Everything I learned everything that helped me to focus, open my eyes, reset my gravity of reference, and practice creativity and think holistically poured out of me in ways I had not experienced in years, if ever, at this magnitude. Truthfully, at the beginning, learning something new and trying to change my life, and writing about it, was all about researching, reading, and reading again and again, as well as interviewing 100 of professionals and meeting new people all the time. With each chapter, however, I found that I was progressively visualizing and thinking like an architect and a designer, and expressing at deeper levels, and applying empathy. I started writing this when I was at Cisco in Las Vegas, traveling from San Francisco for GSX (global sales meeting) in 2015. I wrote with such passion that it took 4 years, and I wrote many more words than I had planned to. I cut over 50,000 words, and some of interviews, from the first draft of my manuscript, which would be just about as long as this final book. The real reason to cut was due to an advancement in technology innovation, to keep changing and adding newer and newer things to make a meaningful book for you. I have kept this book as a digital companion project book for my life, and for many other digital learners of 2 billion under age 20. My creative productivity for myself, and for my corporate friends, colleagues, and family, was supercharged. The energy in my body and spirit was digitized and electrified, and inspired with momentum. I didn't want to stop growing or preaching about architecting your future in the digital era for future transformation. I have fallen in love with learning, and with experiencing myself.

I deeply hope that this book will help you to enjoy the exhilaration of architecting your future in the new digital machine age, and help to disrupt you to be successful in the future.

Best of luck.

Architecting your future has begun now, and you will see a major transformation in yourself by applying the simple methods and technology disrupters in your life, learning, and approach to lead the future.

CONGRATULATIONS!

APPENDIX A
Exploring Activities

EXOLORING ACTIVITY 1.1: SELF GRATITUDE

EXPLORING ACTIVITY 1.2: CAREER /HEALTH//
 FAMILY /RELATINSHIP/FINANCE/ART/
 PLAY (CHFFRFAP SUCEE METER)

EXPLORING ACTIVITY 2.1: PLOTTING YOUR
 FUTURE OF LIFE, CAREER, and WORK &
 DREAM SCALE

EXOLORING ACTIVITY 3.1: CONSTRUCTING YOUR
 ENERGEY AND PERFORMANCE

EXPLORING ACTIVITY 4.1: GOALS, SYSTEM AND
 FOCUS (30G-3P-30M rules)

EXPLORING ACTIVITY 4.2: HEALTH AND FITNESS

EXPLORING ACTIVITY 4.3: SAMPLE HEALTH
 LOGS

EXPLORING ACTIVITY 4.4: RELATIONSHIPS

EXPLORING ACTIVITY 4.5: FINANCE AND
 PERSONAL ECONOMY

EXPLORING ACTIVITY 4.6: FAMILY GOALS

EXPLORING ACTIVITY 4.7: ART AND PLAY GOALS

EXOLORING ACTIVITY 5.1: ARCHITECTURE YOUR
 LIFE

EXPLORING ACTIVITY 6.1: MOTIVATION AND
MOMENTUM

EXPLORING ACTIVITY 7.1: TIME, ENERGY, FOCUS,
SELF-MANAGEMENT

EXPLORING ACTIVITY 8.1: MANAGING ENERGY
AND EMOTION FOR PERFORMANCE

EXPLORING ACTIVITY 9.1: BUILD YOUR INNER
CIRCLE FOR TRANSFORMING YOUR
FUTURE

EXPLORING ACTIVITY 10.1: DIGITAL INDUSTRIES
AND ORGANIZATIONS

EXPLORING ACTIVITY 11.1: DIGITAL CAREER
(DIGIPRENEUR)

EXPLORING ACTIVITY 12.1: 7 TECHNOLOGY
TRANSFORMATION

APPENDIX B
Diagrams

DIAGRAM 1.1   CHFFRFAP – LIFE-SCALE SPEEDO METER

DIAGRAM 1.2   KoK-Leong – ACCESS CURRENT LIFE SUCCESS WHEEL

DIAGRAM 1.3   Dr Raj – ACCESS CURRENT LIFE SUCCESS WHEEL

DIAGRAM 1.4   CAREER SPEEDO METER

DIAGRAM 1.5   HEALTH AND FITNESS SPEEDO METER

DIAGRAM 1.6   FAMILY AND RELATIONSHIP SPEEDO METER

DIAGRAM 1.7   FINANCE SPEEDO METER

DIAGRAM 1.8   ART AND PLAY SPEEDO METER

DIAGRAM 2.1   ARCHITECTURAL THINKING SCALE (DREAM, CAREER AND LIFE-SCALE)

DIAGRAM 2.2   LIFE-SCALE

DIAGRAM 3.1   FOUR SELF-DEVELOPMENT APPROACHES

DIAGRAM 3.2   PHYSIOLOGY AND EMOTION LEADS TO PERFORMANCE

DIAGRAM 3.3   MOMENTUM P-E OWNERSHIP
               GRAPHS

DIAGRAM 3.4   UEDIC MODEL (Understand, Explore,
               Develop, Implement and Confirm)

DIAGRAM 3.5   ARCHITECTING YOUR FUTURE –
               ICT Method

DIAGRAM 3.6   FOUR STEPS TO GROWTH

DIAGRAM 3.7   FOUR STEPS FOR FAST AND
               CURIOUS LEARNING

DIAGRAM 3.8   HIGH PERFORMER LEARNING
               CYCLE

DIAGRAM 3.9   RARE AND VALUABLE SKILLS

DIAGRAM 4.0   GOALS ARE A CHOICE

DIAGRAM 4.1   YOUR GOALS

DIAGRAM 4.2   YOUR GOALS LINK

DIAGRAM 4.3   CAREER PROFESSIONAL DRIVERS

DIAGRAM 4.4   CAREER GOAL SETTING PLAN
               AND PREPARATION STEPS

DIAGRAM 4.5   HEALTH PERFOMANCE SPEEDO
               METER

DIAGRAM 4.6   FOUR STEPS OF FINANCIAL
               GOALS

DIAGRAM 5.1   TALENT STACK PLATFORM

DIAGRAM 5.2   DUAL DEEP COMPETENCY

DIAGRAM 5.3   UDEIC Model

DIAGRAM 5.4   ARCHITECTURAL THINKING
               APPROACH

DIAGRAM 5.5 ARCHITECTURAL THINKING APPROACH (Abhinav's example)

DIAGRAM 7.1 PRODUCTIVITY MODEL

DIAGRAM 7.2 FOCUS FUNNEL

DIAGRAM 7.3 PRODUCTIVITY ON PURPOSE (POP) GRAPHS

DIAGRAM 9.1 INTELLECTUAL INNER CIRCLE

DIAGRAM 9.2 INNER CIRCLE TOWER

DIAGRAM 9.3 TEAM CIRCLE

DIAGRAM 10.1 DUAL DEEP COMPETENCY WITH GROWTH MINDSET

DIAGRAM 10.2 TSP WITH HORIZONTAL SKILLS AND VERTICAL DEVELOPMENT

DIAGRAM 10.3 TECHNOLOGY AND INDUSTRY DISRUPTIONS

DIAGRAM 10.4 DISRUPTIVE CURVE OF TECHNOLOGY

DIAGRAM 10.5 VIRTUAL DIGITAL ERA

DIAGRAM 11.1 DIGIPRENEUR MINDSET

DIAGRAM 12.1 SEVEN FUTURE TECHNOLOGY DISRUPTERS

DIAGRAM SUMMARY AYF IN A PAGE

APPENDIX C
Tables

TABLE 4.1 WHO, WHAT, WHERE, WHEN, AND HOW SUMMARY TABLE

TABLE 4.2 RYAN'S KEY STEPS – ACTION PLAN

TABLE 4.3 7-DAY DAILY ARTISTIC AND PLAYFUL PLAN

TABLE 4.4 DO'S and DON'TS OF GOAL SETTING

TABLE 5.1 TSP-TALENT STACKING PLATFORM TABLE REFERENCE

Glossary

Term	Descriptions
AYF	Architecting your future is an architecture thinking to define your future path.
CHFFRFAP	Career, Health, Finance, Family, Relationship, Family, Art and Play - Seven pillar of your life.
Career-Scale	How you measure your career scale and your desire toward your career
DYF	Design your future is a design thinking process to solve specific problem.
DDC	Double deep competency; Competency with resilient capability, in case one competency absolute then you apply alternative competency and if you combined together you should have rare skills to lead the future
Digipreneur	Entrepreneur with digital skills and mind-sets

Term	Descriptions
Dream Scale	How you measure your dream scale, your desire toward your dream and destiny.
ELP	Energy linked with performance. Energy is source of living positive life with energetic life-style.
TSP	Talent stacking platform- Multiple skills and talent stacked together to be ready for future.
Globtech	Globalization with Technology advancement
Horizontal skills,	Horizontal skills which grow horizontally , example like "EEE"- education, experience and exposer
Inner-Circle	Your circle of influence and association
Life-Scale	How you measure your life scale and your desire toward your life
4Self-CDEF	4Self-CDEF strategy): self-confidence, self-discipline, self-education, and self-reliance, and reflection are the steps to success in digital era.

Term	Descriptions
UEDIC	UEDIC is framework and methodology of architecture thinking. **U = Understanding, E = Exploring, D = Developing, I = Implementing, C = Confirming**
7GT4AYF	7 Global technology for architecting your future.
Vertical development	Vertical development skills which grow in vertical direction and provide you growth and new skills and challenges for a future and its required continues development process. Example: Problem solving, cognitive skills developments, communication development, and relationship and new one digital intelligence.
Emotion	Electromagnetic motion in your body, Consider to be physiological signals to keep your emotion balance

Acknowledgements

"No one who achieves success does so without acknowledging the help of others. The wise and confident acknowledge this help with gratitude."

– Alfred North Withehead

I have been fortunate to work with thousands of people in different companies (Citibank, Cisco, IBM, HPE, BT, NTT, and HPE-Aruba), who keep inspiring me to share the powerful experience of information and communication technology in business, and the experience of being a leader. I acknowledge everyone who inspired me to learn, share my knowledge and experience; hence, I decided to write this book for people who really need inspiration, guidance and support. I have spent endless hours talking to some of you, asking about your career journey and challenges, and how you see the future of technology. Each of you has helped to make this book be successfully written.

Most of the time, when I pick up a book from the bookstore for the first time, I immediately flip to the acknowledgements page. Like many readers, I am always eager to peek behind the curtain, to see the people behind the success and support; I want to meet the cast and crew responsible for the show. If you like this book, please know that credit for its creation is shared among the wonderful human beings recognized here. It's time for these supportive people to step up into the book for a moment and take a well-deserved bow. If I have left anyone in the wings, I apologize; any omissions are inadvertent. Even if "I" is used in this book, it represents "We," as I have written this book based on real research and interviews, debate, discussion based on the "pain and gain" of real life, and the "struggles and joy" in the technology and future digital era.

First and foremost I would like to thank my Papa and Mummy for having trusted me, and for allowing me the independence to choose my career and architect my future. Thanks to my wife Divya Jyoti, my sons Abhinav Aditya and Chinmay Aditya, for filling every day with fun, enjoyment and learning. Your patience, time, motivation, good humor, stories and day-to-day support made this book possible. My in-laws, Sri Baldeo Prasad and Smt Leelawati Singh, you gave us everything for our children, and we love you for that. Divya, you make me a better person every day; this book would not have been written without your support, your work and always willing to listening to my lectures, my research, and tolerating my endless speech. Special thanks to my grandfather, the late Sri Raj Kumar Rai, my grandma and uncles, who always had higher expectations of me than I had of myself, and whose blessing is always with me. Love you, Dada Ji.

Thank you, Hari Prasad, Ramesh Singh sir, and Deepak Singh, Raju Kumar, Sanjay Kumar, Dinesh Singh, for being always teachers and giving me direction.

I want to thank my personal book architect, Naval Kumar, and publisher leader, Liz Ventrella, for all the support, continuous mentoring and guidance. Liz, you are so special, and your support on my author journey is commendable. I'd like to thank my editor, Lisa Browning, for continuously working and putting in more effort than I expected.

My extreme gratitude to Sudesh Shah, for being my buddy who always motivates, guides, and stands by me to provide continuous support. Sanjeev Agarwal, Sudheer Pandita, Vijay Pai, thank you for inspiring me; Prof. Sanjeeva Dube for your review and input when we met in Singapore at SP Jain Management College; Terry John, Terry Shaw, Karim Virani from IBM global outsources project. David Asher, Saurabh Parekh, Shashi Savkur, for being inspiring leaders. Naveen Jaiswal from Japan for patiently listening and giving me input. Kanti, for continuous encouragement and regular input; Dr. Jadish Chinappa, who fights the "what is right?" versus "what is the best" battle every day. You are one of my sources of inspiration and guidance for my book and daily life. Thanks to Navendu Shekhar and Dibeyendu Shekhar, always available to support. Tony Cadelina for always being positive and ready to listen; Sean Geraghty for helping support the IBM EMEA project; Amol Mitra for continuous support and guidance; Rajanikanth for continuously listening and providing advice. Great appreciations to all my friends and students across the globe, for working with me and sharing your pain and gain in developing your future career in advancement of technology. Thanks to my colleagues from Citibank, Cisco, IBM, DXC, NTT, and HPE-Aruba across the world, for making my technological journey so exciting and achieving great adventure and success. Greatest thanks to all my school friends, and my University of Southern Queensland friends for always motivating me to write, and for sharing your "TSP"- talent stacking platform. Suresh kumar Subramanian, Amit Kapoor, Sridhar, Jay, Anwar, Bhaskar, for always motivating and helping me drive the extra mile in life. Rahul Ratnakar and Nilesh from US for providing eye-opening feedback on how to shape up our future in the upcoming digital world.

Some of my special global leaders and colleagues who have always inspired my career, life and dreams: John Chambers, Cisco System, ex-president and CEO, for inspiring my journey to be a network and communication leader; CSR-corporate social responsibility project in India, Jordon, Kenya and South Africa. It has been remarkable learning from you. Vishal Gupta, for mentoring and inspiring me to take more responsibility and grow globally; Sameer Padhye, Kapil Khandelwal, Ramesh Kaza, Ramesh Ramnath, Anil Bhasin, for always inspiring me. Sukhbir Singh Sethi and Ravinder pal Singh, for driving some new initiatives and showing new way learning.

To the forward-thinking leaders at HPE-Aruba, Keerti Melkote, Steve Wood, Carpentier Alain, Adrian Hurel, Campbell Dirk, Justin Chiah, Kapoor Narinder, Guruswami Jambunathan, Anthony Smith, Richard Lim, Devlin Pat Danger, Tanaka Yasuteru-san, Ghose Santanu, Andrew Fox, Nilesh Savkoor, Yokoi Koji-san, Christine Hwang, Amy Sua, Umezu-san and Richard Lim for driving and leading a new way of doing business.

Andy Cheung, for helping me with new assignments. Mr. Gurpreet Singh Ahuja and Abhilash Nair, for always insisting that I take one step ahead in life.

Toastmaster International-Singapore Simei-club's friends and leaders, for motivating me, and supporting me every week to make "Architecting your Future" a reality.

Special acknowledgement to Lee Jin Hwui, DTM, Ramesh, Pravin, Amy, Sandy Lim, Manoj Chugani, Datta Gujjar, Rampreet Sandhu, Justin, Roger, Harsh Goel, Joseph Soh, Junnie Lim, Dave, Rajesh, Saravanan, Vamachi, and Wee Yong.

Thanks to Siva Subramanian, for being a mentor, and motivating me to think beyond career and professional life.

Kishore Babu and Susheela for inspiring me and helping me lead by example; Dr. Sunita Maheswari, CEO of Tele-Red for always motivating me.

Garry Robert, you are my unique teacher. Thank you for supporting me to become an author and writing authority.

Next special acknowledgement to Dr. Linda Ginzel, for teaching "leadership is choice" and foundation of leadership development from Chicago booth.

Finally, to all my global readers. I would like to acknowledge all the readers. In particular, for picking up this book and taking the time to read it. I know you could have selected so many other books to read; however, the fact that you chose this book shows me that you are committed to grow and build your career for a better future, and create a better life for yourself and your loved ones.

I truly wish you every success.

References and Notes

1. World Economic Forum: Skills you need to thrive in the fourth industrial revolution.

2. www.hnkpmgciosurvey.com/charts

3. 4th World Economic Forum 2018

4. NLP, DISC, MBTI, 16PF, Enneagram, Ocean 5, and Pythagoras character development method available for persona development and assessment.

5. http://d-sites.net/english/mimesisplay.html : Description about Play and Art

6. *Designing Your Life*, by Dave Evans and Bill Burnett

7. Dweck, Carol. *Mindset: The New Psychology of Success.* New York: Random house, 2006.

8. https://www.ted.com/talks/andrew_mcafee_what_will_future_jobs_look_like?language=en

9. https://www.daenotes.com/electronics/communication-system/aviation-marine-communication

10. https://www.forbes.com/sites/jacobmorgan/2015/12/16/how-you-define-work/#74e10679198a

11. https://en.wikipedia.org/wiki/Body_fat_percentage

12. https://tanita.eu/tanita-academy/understanding-your-measurements/physique-rating

13. https://en.wikipedia.org/wiki/Bone_density

14. https://www.healthline.com/health/visceral-fat#rating-and-measuremen

15. https://www.theodysseyonline.com/self-determination-constructing-your-own-future

16. https://en.wikipedia.org/wiki/Acetylcholine

17. https://en.wikipedia.org/wiki/Apophenia

18. Bestselling from UK on Leadership and Performance.

    Dr. Alan, Business Leader and Neuro Expert, and TED Speaker.

19. *Designing Your Life*, Bestseller from US, applied the principle from Stanford for last 10 years on design thinking of IBM. Bill and Dave are both TED speakers.

20. Architectural Thinking for Enterprise from IBM

21. *Designing Your Life*, by Dave Evans and Bill Burnett

22. *Vertical Leadership Development – Developing Leaders for a Complex World*, by Nick Petrie

23. http://puttincologneontherickshaw.com/authors-blog/if-you-fail-to-plan-you-plan-to-fail/How to Achieve Your Most Ambitious Goals, Stephen Duneier, TEDxTucson; follow the marginal improvements to achieve bigger goal.

24. https://www.youtube.com/watch?v=TQMbvJNRpLE

25. https://www.thebalance.com/organize-your-finances 1389025?_ga=2.92014297.2101063381.1538843394-20972 54601.1538499133

26. Most important and valuable is relationship:

What keeps us happy and healthy as we go through life? If you think its fame and money, you're not alone but according to psychiatrist, Robert Waldinger, you're mistaken. As the director of the 75-year-old study on adult development, Waldinger has unprecedented access to data on true happiness and satisfaction. In this talk, he shares three important lessons learned from the study, as well as some practical, old-as-the-hills wisdom on how to build a fulfilling, long life.

27. https://www.youtube.com/watch?v=8KkKuTCFvzI

28. https://news.harvard.edu/gazette/story/2017/04/over-nearly-80-years-harvard-study-has-been-showing-how-to-live-a-healthy-and-happy-life/

10 reasons why ART/Play are important for our lives.

29. https://www.theodysseyonline.com/10-reasons-why-arts-are-important-in-our-lives

30. *Measure What Matters*, by John Doerr

31. *Mastery*, by Robert Greene

32. *Emotional Agility*, by Susan David

33. *Coherence: The Secret Science of Brilliant Leadership*, by Alan Watkins

34. https://convertkit.s3.amazonaws.com/landing_pages/incentives/000/463/045/original/Range.pdf?1572823490

35. https://www.davidepstein.com/

How to Learn Anything Fast, by Josh Kaufman, author and business advisor

36. https://www.youtube.com/watch?v=EtJy69cEOtQ

37. *Coherence: The Secret Science of Brilliant Leadership*, by Alan Watkins

38. https://hbr.org/2015/06/the-great-decoupling

39. Seeing Digital: A Visual Guide to the Industries, Organizations, and Careers of the 2020s, by David C.Moschella

40. Concerns about the future of people's well-being.

41. http://www.pewinternet.org/2018/04/17/concerns-about-the-future-of-peoples-well-being/

42. Bureau of Economic Analysis about digital economy impact and GDP report

43. https://www.bea.gov/system/files/papers/WP2018-4.pdf

44. *The Anticipatory Organization*, by Daniel Burrus

Video:

45. Andrew McAfee: MIT: What will future jobs look like?

My all-time choice: Website YouTube video for watch book summary and one page summary

www.ProductivityGame.com by Nathan Lozeron

46. https://hyperledger.github.io/composer/v0.16/tutorials/developer-tutorial

47. http://www.pewinternet.org/2018/04/17/concerns-about-the-future-of-peoples-well-being/

48. Seeing Digital: A Visual Guide to the Industries, Organizations, and Careers of the 2020s, by David C.Moschella

49. https://www.arubanetworks.com/assets/wp/WP_802.11AX.pdf

50. The Anticipatory Organization, by Daniel Burrus

51. The globaltics upheaval ,globalization, robotics, and future of work by Richard Baldwin

52. https://www.windpowerengineering.com/global-iot-market-to-reach-318-billion-by-2023-says-globaldata/

53. https://fourweekmba.com/ai-industry/

54. https://www.marketsandmarkets.com/Market-Reports/3d-printing-market-1276.html?gclid=EAIaIQobChMItdLolLD k5QIVQhh9Ch15eAo4EAAYASAAEgIMdfD_BwE

55. https://www.ibm.com/downloads/cas/PPRR983X

56. https://www.statista.com/statistics/647231/worldwide-blockchain-technology-market-size/

57. https://www.marketsandmarkets.com/Market-Reports/cyber-security-market-505.html?gclid=EAIaIQobChMIx46 43dvk5QIVmQVyCh18KQ_nEAAYASAAEgJxkvD_BwE

58. https://www.globenewswire.com/news-release/2019/04/ 09/1801715/0/en/Global-5G-Market-2019-2025-The-Market-is-Expected-to-Reach-277-Billion-by-2025-at-a-CAGR-of-111-During-2019-2025.html

59. Goals vs System: How to fail and still win big by Sscott Adams

60. https://www.zdnet.com/article/this-is-the-era-of-mone tizing-your-skill-set/

About Ravindar

A warded the Authority in Aspiring Technologist, by *New York Times* bestselling authors, Jack Canfield and Raymond Aaron, Ravindar has been at the forefront of the information and technology sector for more than two decades.

The award-winning author currently work as a leader of services and solution sales for Asia pacific and Japan at HPE-Aruba, lives in Singapore and travels extensively across the world, conducting the Technology Solutions, Services and Sales, as well as being a technology speaker to build integrated, scalable, future-proof technology and business architecture focused on digital technology, strategies, and transformation of businesses globally. Ravindar has worked across multiple verticals and has found the biggest gap between people, technology, and processes, which is strategic planning for any digital technology, specific to Next-Generation Network and Communication being overlooked across the board. He is not just adding technology, but transforming it by increasing efficiency and productivity, while at the same time reducing overall cost by adopting a technology mindset. He has worked with large enterprises and multinational companies with budgets of millions of dollars. Global teams, and much to his surprise, even the big players in any vertical have a tunnel vision focus on just one part of information and technology at all times.

With this book, he has shared his years of experience and in-depth blueprints that have helped many people, businesses across the world to increase their bottom line profits by applying technology, and to decrease their overall costs, all whilst keeping their latest technology future proof and scalable.

He has a Master's degree in Information Science, from USQ Australia, and has pursued a living and passion of excellence in the digital era and technology. He has acquired most of his skills by working in the field with Fortune 100 IT companies around the world.

Ravindar Kumar is an award-winning author and technologist.

Book Ravindar to deliver a keynote address for your organization or technology conference, career & Professional development, and technology innovation. Ravindar knows when, how, and where to motivate and add energy with each specialized technology talk. Participants will engage, learn, connect, and be more conscious of their own digital journey, in the fast, curious, and forward-thinking world.

Keynote topics include:

- Architecting your future in the digital era.
- Why technologists triumph in the generalist world
- Talent stacking platform for students and professionals in the digital era

- Architectural thinking and role of enterprise architect
- WI-FI for the future
- Promise of networks in the digital era.
- Seven technology disrupters for architecting your future -7GT4AYF
- **Energy link with performance**: The heart generates 5000 times more energy than the brain, but we still follow the *brain power.*

Book online at:
Architectingyourfuture.com
OR
Email address: AYF@architectingyourfuture.com

Download your bonus website:
www.architectingyourfuture.com

Made in the USA
Monee, IL
09 June 2020

32620106R00193